PICKER'S
POCKET·GUIDE

COMIC BOOKS

How to Pick Antiques like a Pro

DAVID TOSH

Published by

Krause Publications, a division of F+W Media, Inc.
700 East State Street • Iola, WI 54990-0001
715-445-2214 • 888-457-2873
www.krausebooks.com

To order books visit us online at www.krausebooks.com

Cover photos top row, from left: *Action Comics* #1—see P. 6, 8, 13, 36, 37, 161-169; Four Color #386 *Uncle Scrooge* (Dell, 1952), CGC NM 9.4, one of the most important Disney comics and counts as *Uncle Scrooge* #1, **$28,680**; *Journey into Mystery* #83—see P. 102, 114, 170; **bottom row, from left:** *Captain America* #2— see P. 74; *Sensation Comics* #1 (DC, 1942), CGC NM 9.4, continuation of Wonder Woman's origin story from her first appearance in *All Star Comics* #8, **$83,650**; *Green Lantern* #76—see P. 123; *Batman* #9 (DC, 1942), CGC NM 9.4, includes the first Batman Christmas story and a story featuring The Joker, **$28,680**.
Back cover photos top row, from left: *Tales of Suspense*—see P. 100; *Cerebus the Aardvark* #1—see P. 135; *Conan the Barbarian* #1—see P. 127; **bottom row, from left:** *Showcase* #4 *The Flash*—see P. 80; *Archie Comics* #1— see P. 64; *Amazing Fantasy* #15—see P. 113.

ISBN-13: 978-1-4402-4498-8
ISBN-10: 1-4402-4498-7

Designed by: Jana Tappa
Edited by: Kristine Manty

Printed in China

10 9 8 7 6 5 4 3 2 1

CONTENTS

Foreword

They say the Golden Age of Comic Books is the most influential of them all. No argument here. But growing up in the 1980s had more than its fair share of milestones still relevant today. It was a grand time to be a comic book reader: *Watchmen. Dark Knight Returns. Batman: Year One.* First Comics' *Teenage Mutant Ninja Turtles.* DC's *Crisis.* Newsstand books were 75 cents (as a Michigan kid that was equal to seven returnable aluminum cans plus a nickel from my dad's bowl of change). By the 1980s, everyone owned a healthy stack of comics; and in 1986, I turned 10 years old.

That was the year I wanted nothing more than to get into the comic book shop. That's where the real stories were – the weighty ones. The types of stories my parents did not want me to read. This, of course, meant I wanted to read them even more.

By the time the 1990s rolled in, my attention span for comics was displaced (somewhat, never fully) by girls, high school, and summer jobs. Something changed about the comics then, too. Suddenly every copy became a "Collector's Edition." Slick covers were accented with diecut-limited edition-foil-five variants-lenticular special effects. You didn't have to wait decades for your favorite books to increase in value - it only took weeks. By 1995, it seemed Beanie Babies and four-year-old copies of *X-Men* #1 were in a cage match to see which one could quadruple in value by the end of the summer. At least, that's what we were told.

If you think the after effects of a decade-long trend in "insta-values" died with the Clinton administration, then this book is exactly what you need to learn the difference between a six-figure comic book and a reading copy. Headline-grabbing sales of multi-million dollar comic book auctions and a decade's worth of reality TV make people wonder: "What are my comics worth?"

That's why David Tosh is the best person to write a book like this. David has witnessed the trends, the characters, the marketing ploys, and the economics behind the comics collecting hobby ebb and flow for decades. It's not always easy to separate the best from the rest, but that's what David does day in and day out.

Not only has he seen the rise in million dollar comics, he's held them in his hands and described them with accuracy and enthusiasm for the education and enjoyment of layman and fanboy alike. David's desk is the landing pad for some of the most valuable comic books, animation art, and original comic art to have been sold in recent years.

When I was cracking the door on the comic book shop, it was fans like David who welcomed me in. They were excited to share what they learned. Years later, the generation they mentored turned fandom into a cultural movement. I can't help but think how lucky we are for the opportunity to jump inside his world and his passion … and this book is the diving board.

— Eric Bradley
Dallas, Texas
May 15, 2015

Introduction

"Superman's *Action Comics* #1 Sells for $3.2 Million."

That much money for a *comic book*? One that originally sold for a dime? C'mon!

It's true. In the past ten years, certain vintage American comic books have soared in value, with several different comic books trading hands for over a million dollars. How can this be? Aren't comic books just for kids? Not any more, it seems. These days, savvy investors have been eyeing the comic book market like never before. While the stock market endured drastic dips during the recession years of 2008-2010, most blue chip comic books have continued to climb in value. And even though more people than ever before are hot on their trail, amazing collections of 1930s-60s comics keep getting discovered.

With hit movies based on classic comic book characters filling theaters all over the country, attention to this once humble, throw-away form of entertainment has risen every year. What was once a small gathering of Southern California comic fans to buy, sell, and trade, and meet a few comic book professionals, the San Diego Comic-Con has become one of the most important annual media events in the world, drawing hundreds of thousands of fans from all corners of the globe for four days of frantic fun. And San Diego is only one of many cons held each year in all parts of the country and abroad.

The reasons people like to collect comic books are as many and varied as there are different kinds of comics. In the early years, it was for one basic reason: to read them. With so many titles and issues to choose from, most kids could only afford to buy a few new comics off the stands, and then rely on their friends to trade

Doom Patrol #99 (DC, 1965), VF+, is an example of a comic that currently sells for over guide, due to the introduction of a character (Beast Boy, aka Changeling) featured on the popular animated *Teen Titans* TV series, **$54.05**.

for ones that they missed. As the young fans grow up, nostalgia becomes a factor, and it then became a matter of tracking down old favorites in second-hand shops. In time, comic book dealers began to advertise back issues in advertisements placed in the back pages of new comics, which led to the first comic conventions in the 1960s. With the wild success of the *Batman* TV series in 1966, more people than ever became interested, and the age of the serious collector took off.

While the condition of an old comic book – the amount of visible handling wear on the covers first, with the suppleness and brightness of the inside paper secondary – has always been a major factor in determining value, it's never been as important as now. Like coins and sports cards before them, comic books can now be submitted to a third-party grading company to be certified and encapsulated in a hard plastic shell (meaning you can no longer open the pages and read the book). The difference between one point, or even a fraction of a point, can mean thousands of dollars for certain comic books.

But that doesn't necessarily mean all old comic books are valuable – and this book is designed to help the "lay" collector in identifying comic books with value, and those with little value. You may be surprised just how many old comic books are worth very little. Keep in mind that for many years, comic books were hugely popular and inexpensive forms of entertainment, aimed at the masses. It

The author, holding a copy of *Detective Comics* #27 (first appearance of Batman, 1939), which sold for over one million dollars!

wasn't unusual for some titles to sell over a million copies month after month. In fact, more old comic books were saved throughout the years than you might have thought. Problem with most of those saved books is that they are in pretty rough shape today, due to lack of proper storage and excessive handling. But there were a few farsighted individuals that, for whatever reason, saved hordes of comics, some in the most ideal conditions.

The most famous horde of comics found to date was the" Mile High Collection" discovered in Denver, Colorado, in 1977. The collection had been owned by a late graphic artist named Edgar Church, who from 1937 to 1955 bought a copy of just about every comic ever published, including *Action Comics* #1 and lots of other key issues. Mr. Church kept most of his collection in a cedar-lined basement, where they stayed extremely well preserved. After Mr. Church passed away, his heirs sold them to Chuck Rozanski, owner of a small chain of Denver comic shops. This incredible horde helped kick-start the modern era of comic book collecting, with condition now a driving factor. The biggest collectors competed for the few truly high-grade copies available, and prices begin to skyrocket. And as prices rose, more hordes began to surface.

Today, most high end comic books are sold by auction companies like Heritage Auctions. In the twelve years I've worked for Heritage, I've seen some amazing comic books come through, like a high-grade copy of *Detective*

Police Comics #1 Mile High pedigree, (Quality, 1941), CGC NM 9.4. This comic from the legendary Edgar Church collection contains the first appearance of Plastic Man, as well as the first appearances of Phantom Lady, Firebrand, and the Human Bomb, **$31,070**.

Comics #27, featuring the first appearance of Batman. It had been purchased used in the 1960s or early 70s for the going rate of the time; when Heritage sold the copy in 2010, it sold for $1,075,500.00 – the first comic book sold at auction to bring over a million. Not all comics are best served by a big auction house, though, and for many lesser value books, eBay and other internet services have been good ways to sell. We'll cover other ways to make a profit selling comics later in the book.

Back in the 1990s, when I ran a small collectibles shop in Arkansas, I spent plenty of time on the road, on the lookout for any interesting small antique stores, yard sales, and the like, stocking items for my customers. I've found great comics in out-of-the-way flea markets, small one-day collectibles fairs, garage sales, and all points in-between. I've made more than a few mistakes, but worked my way up to a position at the Comics and Comic Art Division of Heritage Auctions, where I've managed to help bring in lots of great material from consignors, and have advised many more on best ways to sell, when their collection didn't quite meet Heritage's requirements. It's time for me to pass a little of that experience on to you.

So when you're out in the field picking, keep this little book handy. There's nothing like a little knowledge to get you ahead of the pack!

A note about the photos: Unless otherwise noted, all photos in the book are courtesy of Heritage Auctions.

Action Comics #242 (DC, 1958), uncertified VF. First appearance of Brainiac and the shrunken city of Kandor, Curt Swan cover, Al Plastino and Jim Mooney interior art, **$2,390**.

CHAPTER 1

The Basics

In order to understand comic book collecting, let's take a look at some of the most important trends over the years. Comic books as we know them today began as giveaway editions that reprinted newspaper comic strips. There had been reprint books featuring comic strips since the beginning of the 20th century, but these were more in a "book" format. The first pamphlet-style comics, printed on cheap pulp paper with a cover printed on slick stock or heavier paper, saddle-stitched (stapled) into a booklet measuring roughly 7 inches x 10 inches, began in 1933. The main goal for the publishers at the time was to keep expensive four-color presses running around the clock. The first titles were *A Century of Comics* and *Famous Funnies – A Carnival of Comics*, both published in 1933. One publisher experimented by putting a ten-cent sticker on a stack of one of the giveaways, and placing them on a newsstand; when they quickly sold out, an industry was born.

Soon there were a number of companies churning out comic books featuring familiar strips like *Little Orphan Annie, Terry and the Pirates, Tarzan*, and many more. When publishers began to run out of material to reprint, artists and writers were hired to produce new features. National Allied Publications is the company generally credited with being the first to produce a comic with all new material: the oversized *New Fun: The Big Comic Magazine* #1, in 1935. Their next innovation was *Detective Comics* #1, cover dated March 1937. This was a standard-sized comic, 68 pages including slick covers, and featured "hard-boiled detective" stories starring characters like Speed Saunders and Slam Bradley. The title proved so popular that the publisher became known as DC Comics ("DC" for Detective Comics).

DC then changed everything with an adventure story anthology, *Action Comics*, cover dated June 1938. Issue number one introduced Superman. Soon after this iconic debut, an entire horde of colorfully-costumed "mystery men" comics began flooding the newsstands. Batman was introduced in *Detective Comics* #27, cover dated May 1939. The first issue of *Marvel Comics* (retitled *Marvel Mystery Comics* with issue #2) appeared in late 1939, introducing The Human Torch and The Sub-Mariner. The Golden Age of Comics began.

World War II had a significant impact on the production of comics. Paper rationing caused the page count to drop from 68 to 36 in 1943; this date was considered by early collectors as the end of the True Golden Age. Also, comics were popular with servicemen stationed overseas, causing thousands of comic books to leave the country, most never to be seen again.

After the war, tastes changed, and most of the "second-string" superhero comics vanished (DC's "Big Three," Superman, Batman, and Wonder Woman, survived with their titles intact). The new trend was for Crime, with *Crime Does Not Pay* a huge seller. Where the earlier *Detective Comics* focused on lawmen, these new comics centered on criminals, and excessive violence and bloodshed became commonplace. As the 1940s ended, a new upstart company, EC, took this bloody format even further with a line of Horror Comics like *Tales From The Crypt*. Sales of these types of comics soared, with more publishers upping the ante by attempting to outdo the other for horrific content. It didn't take long for concerned parents and teachers to decry Horror and Crime comic books, resulting in massive roundups of comics in public book burnings. The result was the advent of the Comics Code

GRADING 101

When it comes to determining the value of a comic book, the condition is one of the most important things. I'm referring to the *amount of visible handling wear* on the covers more than anything else. While the condition of the inside pages is important, too, don't worry so much about the color of the paper. I hear time and time again, "Well, the pages are yellow," whenever I ask someone on the phone about condition. Unless the inside pages are turning brown and beginning to crumble around the edges ("brittleness"), don't worry about the color of the paper.

Comics are graded by condition on a scale of .5 to 10. Here's a list of the primary grades:

0.5 Poor (PR): Trashed, incomplete, water damaged, tattered. Basically worthless, unless some of the inner pages are nice enough to "harvest" and be used to fill in an incomplete copy.

1.0 Fair (FR): Heavily read but all there ("beat but complete" is how I used to describe the condition when I was selling old comics). Very little value generally speaking, but could still be worth good money if a key issue like *Action Comics* #1.

2.0 Good (GD): Not bad, but well-read. A well-used copy.

4.0 Very Good (VG): An average used comic, complete but with obvious handling wear. A "not too bad" copy.

6.0 Fine (FN): Above average, with only minor wear along the outer edges and spine.

8.0 Very Fine (VF): Exceptional copy; fresh-looking but with maybe one or two very minor defects, like a rounded corner or tiny scuff.

9.0 Very Fine/Near Mint (VF/NM): Very clean and fresh, maybe one tiny defect.

9.2 Near Mint Minus (NM-): Like new – the highest grade listed in the *Overstreet Comic Book Price Guide*.

The criteria for these higher grades will generally take an expert to determine:

9.4 Near Mint (NM)

9.6 Near Mint Plus (NM+)

9.8 Near Mint/Mint (NM/MT)

9.9 Mint (MT)

10 Gem Mint (GM)

Authority in 1954, placing a large "Approved" stamp in the upper corner of comic book covers; without that approval, news dealers refused to carry them. Comic books without that postage stamp seal in the upper right corner are now referred to as Pre-Code comics.

In the 1950s, the popularity of the syndicated TV series, *The Adventures of Superman*, brought about the revival of many old characters. *Showcase* #4, from DC Comics, reintroduced The Flash in an updated version of the 1940s hero; this issue is generally considered the beginning of The Silver Age of Comics. Marvel, then trading under the name Atlas, spent the fifties churning out monster, war, and romance comics, with one brief return to superheroes in 1953 that died out by '55.

The 1960s saw tremendous growth in comic collecting in general, and superheroes in particular. Fanzines, self-published amateur magazines devoted to comics, started appearing in 1960, which ushered in the age of serious collecting. Pop artists like Andy Warhol and Roy Lichtenstein began using images inspired by comics. The ABC-TV *Batman* series, launched in January 1966, blew the lid off completely, and suddenly everyone seemed to be buying and collecting comics. With the hobby becoming so popular, back issue sale prices began to rise, and comic book dealers began opening shops. Big conventions popped up in major cities, where fans could converge, meet artists and writers, and buy back issues from the ever-growing list of dealers.

During the 1970s' "Bronze Age" period, comic book shops were becoming commonplace in most metropolitan areas and carried just about everything, with unsold copies becoming back issue stock. This led to the independent distribution of comics to stores, with no return policy. This was a pretty big deal, as the old system allowed the sellers to tear off the upper third of the cover (with the title) of unsold comics and return them to the distributor for credit. The Modern Age of Comics (and collecting) had begun!

CARE AND STORAGE

You should have on hand bags and boards to protect the comics you find. By "bag," I'm referring to professionally made poly sleeves, available in a number of sizes. You should have Golden Age and Silver Age sizes. The backing boards are white acid-free sheets of cardboard, designed to fit in the bag with the comic. Don't attempt to do any cleaning or repair any tears – it's important to keep the comic in its original condition (see Chapter 10, Restoration and Repair).

GRADING AT A GLANCE

Proper grading of comic books is difficult, and requires an expert eye. A better way to get an idea of grade while in the field is to use a simpler system:

BAD: See "Poor." Worthless to most collectors.

HEAVILY USED: Comics that are for the most part complete, but tattered from heavy use. Can have small pieces missing from the covers, but must have all pages intact. The corresponding grades would be Fair 1.0 to Good Plus 2.5.

AVERAGE USED: The most common condition for older books. Well-read but complete and sound, cover fully attached. The spine area, especially around the staples, will show wear and minor color loss. Corners may be rounded or creased. There may be writing on the cover, but usually no more than a name. Corresponding grades would be Good/Very Good 3.0 to Fine Minus 5.5.

ABOVE AVERAGE: Obviously read but well-kept, with few small cover flaws like very light stains or small creases. Some handling wear will be apparent, usually along the spine. A nice copy. Corresponding grades are Fine 6.0 to Very Fine 8.0

EXCEPTIONAL: Almost like-new, with only the smallest of flaws and light handling. Corresponding grades are Very Fine Plus 8.5 to Very Fine/Near Mint 9.0

LIKE NEW: Looks as if it were never read, bought brand new and put away for a saver copy. Corresponding grades are Near Mint Minus 9.2 to Mint 10.

ANATOMY OF A COVER

It's surprising to me how many people cannot "read" the cover of a comic book. With collectors, the issue number is extremely important. As an eight-year-old child, I knew to look for the issue number on the front cover, but today this seems to be difficult for many novice collectors to figure out. I get calls almost every day from people who have found an "old" comic, and when I ask them what issue they have, the most common response is, "Where will I find that?" Even worse are those who see the number and month listed, and misunderstand. I've had more than one caller tell me they have found a copy of *Fantastic Four* from the 1940s. Since this particular title began in 1961, this couldn't be true, I tell them. Of course, what they are seeing as "March 48" does not mean the comic was published in 1948 – that "48" is the issue number. Most comics (but not all) do feature the issue number on the front cover. Many Marvel Comics also have a second, smaller-sized number printed on the cover as well; this is a five-digit number beginning with "0" – this number is important only to the publisher, but it's often mistaken as the issue number. And that term should be called "issue" number, not "volume" number (another common mistake).

Let's look at a typical 1970s comic book – *Amazing Spider-Man* #148, cover dated September, 1975:

This is the title of the comic book. Note that it says, "The Amazing" – that's part of the title (not just "Spider-Man").

In some cases, the title of the story also appears, usually along the bottom of the front cover. If you were referring to this comic in conversation with a collector or dealer, you would say, *Amazing Spider-Man #148*. No real need to mention the month or story title.

MARVEL COMICS GROUP™

This is the company name, not the name of the comic book.

The Amazing Spider-Man #148 (Marvel, 1975), FN/VF. Professor Warren revealed as the Jackal, Gwen Stacy clone and Tarantula appearances, cover by Gil Kane and John Romita Sr., with interior art by Ross Andru, **$13**.

Here, "Spider Man" denotes the CHARACTER, not the title (this may change from issue to issue; correct spelling is actually "Spider-Man" with a hyphen.

To the lower left is the cover price ("25¢"). The large 148 is the issue number, under that is the issue's cover date month (Note: this is NOT when the comic was sold; in most cases, the month listed is the latest the comic may remain on the stands. They actually come out two to three months earlier).

The odd logo made up of three "C"s is a company name, while the five digit number 02457 is important only to the distributor.

Mickey Mouse Magazine #1 (K. K. Publications/ Western Publishing Co., 1935), FN. Historically, this is one of the most important comic publications ever, with the title eventually morphing into a more "traditional" style comic book in 1940, occasioned by a title change to *Walt Disney's Comics and Stories*. In 1935, it was more an activities book, with puzzles, games, cels, stories, and comics of Disney characters. It was a large format, 13-1/4" x 10-1/4", and used as a promotional magazine for Disney cartoon movies and paraphernalia, $3,346.

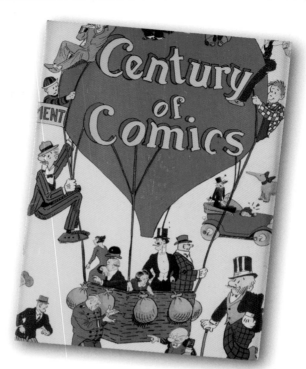

New Comics #4 (DC, 1936), CGC NM- 9.2. Cover is by Vincent Sullivan, highlights include a *Federal Men* story by Jerry Siegel and Joe Shuster (who would go on to create Superman), several features drawn by Sheldon Mayer, and a partial adaptation of Charles Dickens' *A Tale of Two Cities*, **$7,762.50**.

Century of Comics #nn (Eastern Color, 1933), CGC FN- 5.5. Generally recognized as the third comic book, this was distributed as a premium giveaway by Wheatena, Malt-O-Milk, Kinney Shoes, and others, **$4,331.88**.

Superman #1 (DC, 1939), CGC FR 1.0. This issue's cover by Joe Shuster is one of the most famous covers of the Golden Age, **$16,730**.

Detective Comics #31 (DC, 1939), CGC GD 2.0. Has one of the most classic covers in the history of comics and it's just the fifth appearance of Batman. Cover art by Bob Kane and Jerry Robinson, **$34,655**.

64 PAGES OF Thrill-Packed ACTION
SEPTEMBER, 1939
Detective Comics
10¢
Powerful and awesome, the mysterious BATMAN again appears to oppose the evil forces of a terrifying master of crime known as THE MONK!

More Fun Comics #52 (DC, 1940), CGC FN 6.0.
One of the ten most valuable comic books is the key
issue shown here, the origin and first appearance
of the Spectre. His debut story was written by
Jerry Siegel (Superman's co-creator), and drawn by
Bernard Baily, **$65,725**.

World's Best Comics #1 (DC, 1941), CGC FN/VF 7.0.
The reason why there's no issue #1 of *World's Finest*
is because the premiere issue was *World's Best*! The
cover is by Fred Ray, and at that time, it was a novelty
to see Batman and Superman together, **$6,572.50**.

Adventure Comics #55, (DC, 1940), CGC NM/MT 9.8. Bernard Baily cover and interior art, with Creig Flessel also contributing on the interior, **$20,315.**

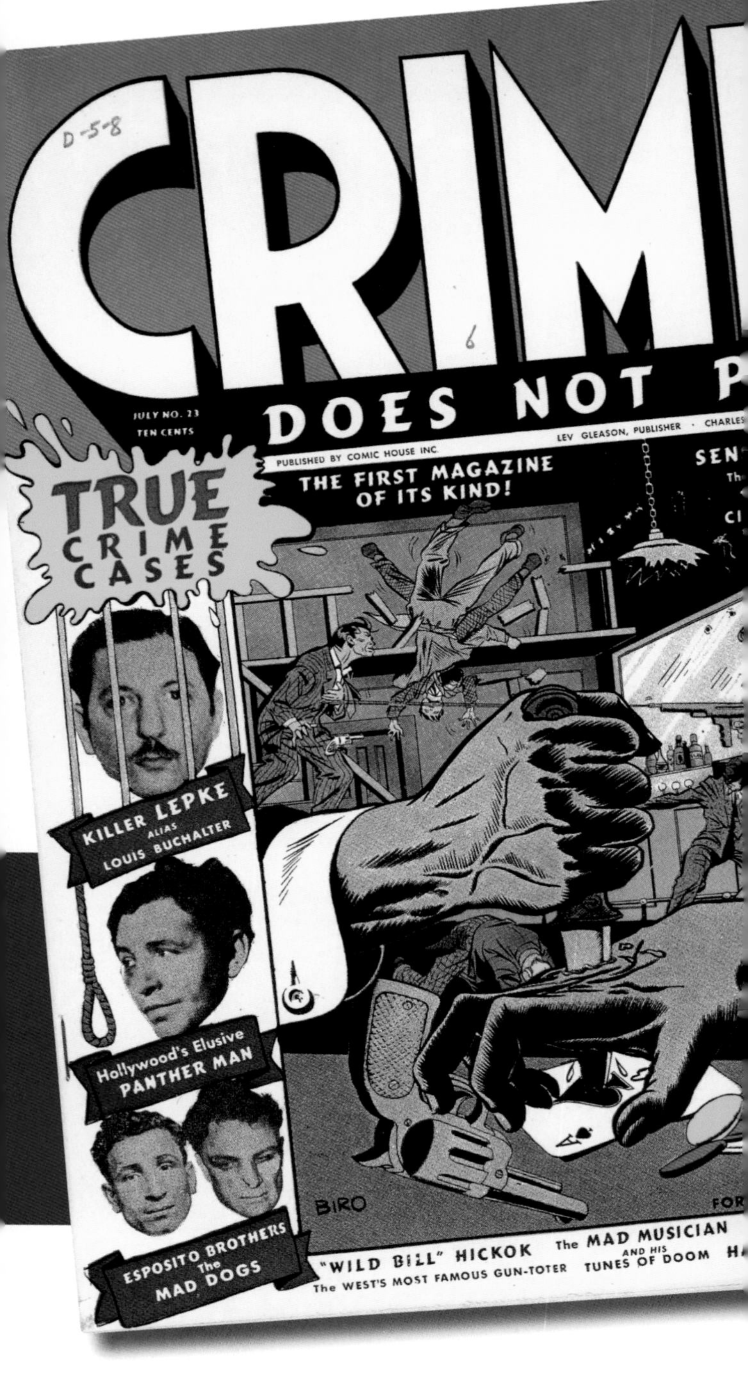
D-5-8
CRIM
DOES NOT P
JULY NO. 23
TEN CENTS
LEV GLEASON, PUBLISHER · CHARLES
PUBLISHED BY COMIC HOUSE INC.
THE FIRST MAGAZINE OF ITS KIND!
TRUE CRIME CASES
KILLER LEPKE ALIAS LOUIS BUCHALTER
Hollywood's Elusive PANTHER MAN
ESPOSITO BROTHERS The MAD DOGS
BIRO
"WILD BILL" HICKOK
The WEST'S MOST FAMOUS GUN-TOTER
The MAD MUSICIAN AND HIS TUNES OF DOOM

All Winners Comics #1 (Timely, 1941), CGC NM+ 9.6. A great cover featuring all of the best Timely characters and also significant because of the Stan Lee-penned text feature with the first appearance of the All-Winners Squad, the first Timely/Marvel superhero group, **$83,650**.

Crime Does Not Pay #22 (Lev Gleason, 1942), NM-. It simply does not get better than this for the crime comic collector. This is the *Action* #1 of crime, the book that started an enormously successful genre. The inside cover trumpets "A Completely New Kind of Magazine" and tells readers, "Criminals are not heroes, they are not even brave or 'nervy'— they are cowardly rats. Sooner or later they get their just reward. Their fate is prison and death," **$11,950**.

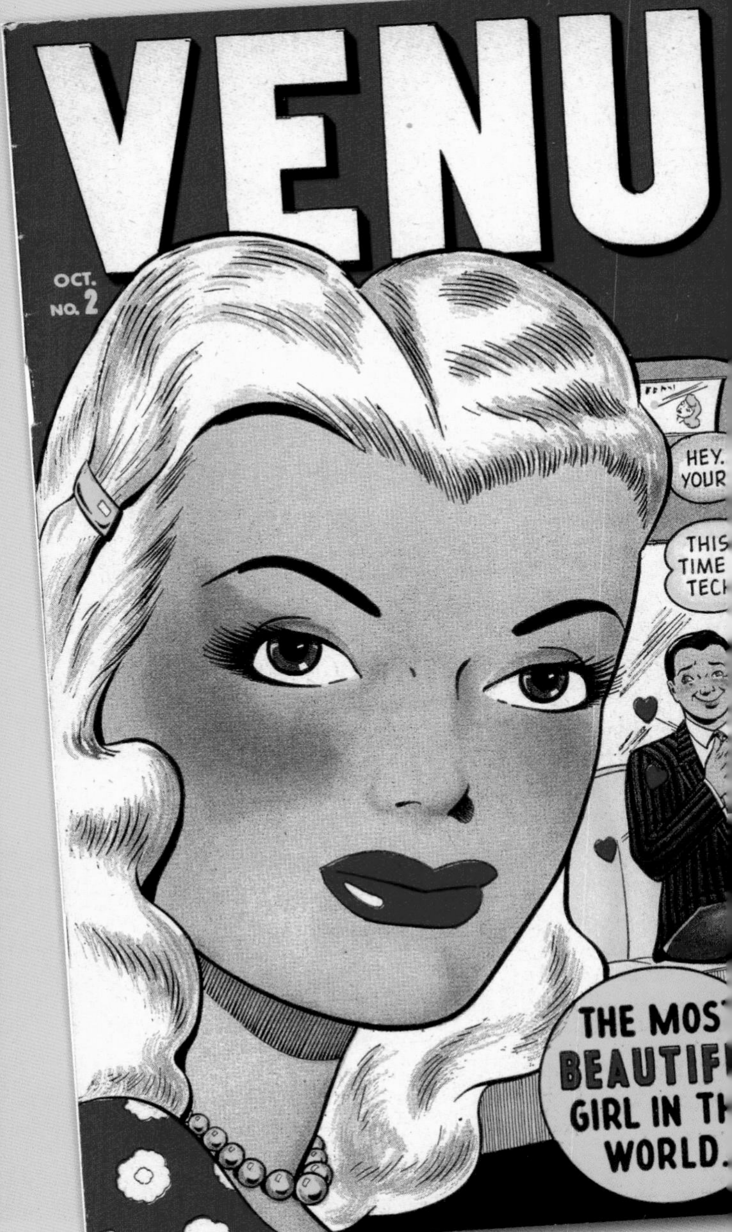
VENU
OCT.
NO. 2
HEY.
YOUR
THIS
TIME
TECH
THE MOST
BEAUTIF
GIRL IN TH
WORLD.

Venus #2 (Atlas, 1948), VF/NM, **$2,629**.

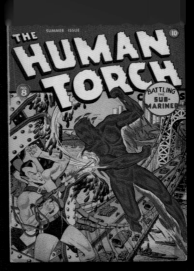

The Human Torch #8 (Timely, 1942),
uncertified, VG. Human Torch vs.
Sub-Mariner battle issue, Hitler
appearance, Alex Schomburg cover,
Basil Wolverton, Allen Simon, Harry
Sahle, and Al Gabriele art, **$1,523.63**.

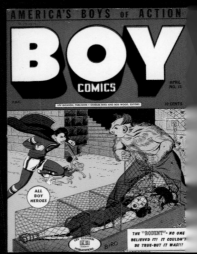

Boy Comics #15 (Lev Gleason, 1944),
uncertified NM-. Cover by Charles Biro.
$2,270.50.

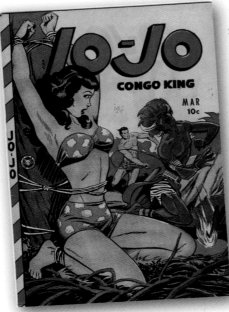

Jo-Jo Comics #25 (Fox Features Syndicate, 1949), uncertified FN. Matt Baker bondage cover, **$717**.

Green Lantern #3 (DC, 1960), GD-. Mart Nodell cover and art, **$258.75**.

Justice League of America #1 (DC, 1960), CGC VG 4.0. Origin and first appearance of Despero; Aquaman, Batman, Flash, Green Lantern, J'onn J'onzz, Superman, and Wonder Woman also appear, Murphy Anderson cover, Mike Sekowsky art, **$507.88**.

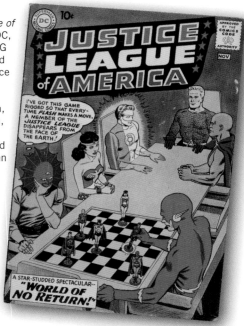

Fantastic Four #1 (Marvel, 1961), Poor. Origin and first appearance of the Fantastic Four, Marvel's first superhero team; origin and first appearance of Mole Man, cover and art by Jack Kirby, **$430.20**. See what a Near Mint-graded copy is worth on P. 111.

▶ *Weird Fantasy* #14 (EC, 1952), CGC VF/NM 9.0. Al Williamson's first published work for E.C, Al Feldstein story and cover, Frank Frazetta/Al Williamson (first team-up at EC), Jack Kamen, Joe Orlando, and Wally Wood art, **$507.88**.

X-Men #8 (Marvel, 1964), CGC VF 8.0. First appearance of Unus the Untouchable, contains a Beast pin-up, Mastermind appearance, Jack Kirby cover and art, **$227.50**.

Iron Man and Sub-Mariner #1 (Marvel, 1968), CGC NM 9.4. Gene Colan and Bill Everett cover, Colan and Johnny Craig art, Iron Man story continued from *Tales of Suspense* #99 and continues in *Iron Man* #1; Sub-Mariner story continued from *Tales to Astonish* #101 and continues in *Sub-Mariner* #1, **$717**.

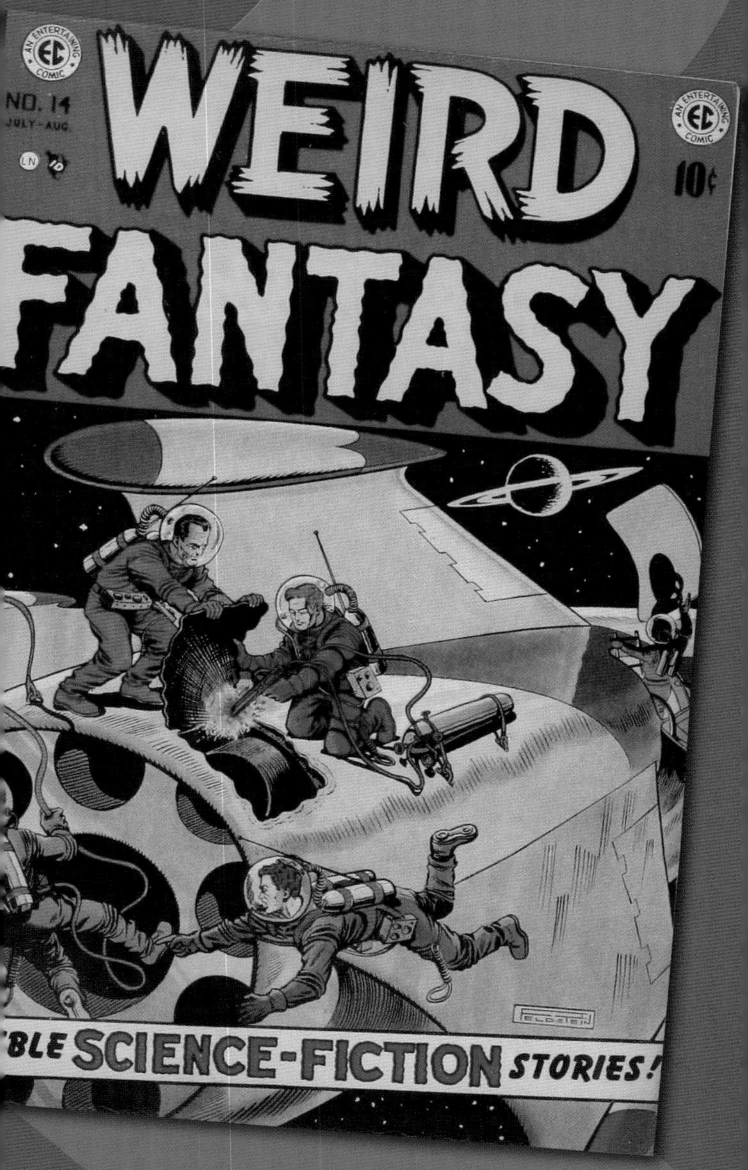
AN ENTERTAINING COMIC EC
NO. 14
JULY-AUG
WEIRD FANTASY
10¢
AN ENTERTAINING COMIC EC
FELDSTEIN
BLE SCIENCE-FICTION STORIES!

X-Men #156 (Marvel, 1982), CGC MT 10.0, Gem Mint copy, Dave Cockrum cover art, **$2,868**.

The Amazing Spider-Man #252 (Marvel, 1984), CGC MT 9.9. It's the issue everyone remembers, with Spider-Man donning his new black costume for the first time, **$5,078.75**.

Famous Funnies (Series 1) #1 (Eastern Color, 1934), CGC GD 2.0. The first comic book actually sold to the public is now one of the steepest challenges for the comic book collector, as only 35,000 were printed, and it's estimated that perhaps ten copies exist, **$7,767.50**.

CHAPTER 2

The 1930s

The dawn of American comic books was in 1933, when newsstand comic books were first produced and sold. The first comic books contained only reprints of newspaper comic strips. As the supply of available strips for reprinting dwindled, art studios began creating new content, with art and original stories that became longer, but still broken up into panels like in the newspapers; this is when the industry really began to take off. Here's a rundown of the important publishers of the 1930s:

EASTERN COLOR

The first regularly scheduled comic book was *Famous Funnies*, produced by Eastern Color. In 1933, they produced a giveaway comic for Gulf Service Stations, called *Gulf Comic Weekly*; this was a four-page tabloid size (10-1/2 inches x 15 inches) comic that mimicked the Sunday papers, only with all-new content. After a name change to *Gulf Funny Weekly*, it ran as a tabloid until 1939, when it adopted a standard comic book format.

More giveaways followed, including *Famous Funnies: a Carnival of Comics*; *A Century of Comics*, and *Skippy's Own Book of Comics*, the first modern comic book devoted to a single character. But it was the *Famous Funnies* title that really got the ball rolling; the first issue was titled *Famous Funnies: Series One*. This was the first 10 cent comic book. The regular *Famous Funnies* series began with a new issue #1, cover dated July 1934. While mostly composed of reprints, there were a few new features created especially for this title. *Buck Rogers* strip reprints were originally the most popular feature; they began with issue #3. All early issues of *Famous Funnies* are tough to find, with issue #2 considered rare.

DC COMICS

This important publisher began as National Allied Publications. Their first title was the tabloid-sized *New Fun: The Big Comic Magazine*, in 1935. The second DC title was *New Comics*, which began late in 1935, as a standard-format comic book. The title evolved into *Adventure Comics*, which ran for many years. Both *New Fun* and *New Comics* featured all-new content, rather than strip reprints.

The third DC comic is what gave the company its name: *Detective Comics*. Issue one was cover dated March, 1937. This was one of the first anthology comics to be devoted to crime fighters, a theme that proved to be wildly popular. But it's the fourth DC title that makes headlines today: *Action Comics* #1, which introduced Superman, the first real costumed crime fighter in comic

TOP 10 1930s COMICS*

1. **ACTION COMICS #1** (FIRST APPEARANCE OF SUPERMAN)

2. **DETECTIVE COMICS #27** (FIRST APPEARANCE OF BATMAN)

3. **SUPERMAN #1**

4. **MARVEL COMICS #1** (FIRST APPEARANCE OF THE HUMAN TORCH)

5. **ACTION COMICS #7**

6. **DETECTIVE COMICS #31**

7. **DETECTIVE COMICS #29**

8. **ACTION COMICS #2**

9. **ACTION COMICS #10**

10. **ADVENTURE COMICS #40**

*BY VALUE

books. With *Detective Comics* #27, the company scored another home run with the introduction of Batman. Soon, cape-wearing characters with secret identities would dominate the comic book scene.

Other DC titles of the 1930s include *More Fun, All-American Comics, New York World's Fair Comics*, and in 1939, the first issue of *Superman*.

DELL COMICS

This big publishing company had experimented with tabloid comics as early as 1929, but it was 1938 when they became affiliated with Western Publishing (aka Western Printing and Lithography), producing titles like *The Funnies, Crackajack Funnies*, and *Super Comics*. Dell was quick to jump on the superhero bandwagon, introducing "mystery men" characters like Phantasmo and The Owl. However, it was the company's series of "one-shot" comics titled *Four Color Comics* that were the most impressive of their 1930s output; each issue was devoted to a different character. The series began in 1939.

Action Comics #1 (DC, 1938), CGC GD/VG 3.0. An unrestored copy of the first appearance of Superman is what most every collector has at the top of his or her want list. This is the most valuable comic issue in the entire hobby, not only because it is the first appearance of Superman, one of the greatest comic characters, but also because this June 1938 issue started the Golden Age of comics. The classic cover by Joe Shuster is also perhaps the most famous comic cover of all time. In August 2014, a pristine copy sold for over $3.2 million. This copy sold at Heritage Auctions for **$310,700**.

FOX FEATURE SYNDICATE (FOX COMICS/FOX PUBLICATIONS)

Fox Comics began as the brain child of Victor Fox, said to have been a former accountant at DC who was so impressed with that company's sales figures he started his own business. His company's first big title was *Wonder Comics*, starring Wonder Man, a superhero character so closely resembling Superman that a lawsuit brought him down after his first (and only) appearance. Other Fox titles included *Mystery Men Comics* (August 1939), *Fantastic Comics* (December 1939), and *Blue Beetle* (Winter 1939).

CENTAUR PUBLICATIONS

In 1936, publisher Everett "Busy" Arnold published his first comic, *The Comics Magazine* (May 1936) as part of his Comics Magazine Company. This title introduced the very first masked hero in American comics, The Clock. Meanwhile, Harry "A" Chesler brought out *Star Comics* and *Star Ranger* (both dated February 1937) under the imprint Chesler Publications. Both titles, along with *The Comics Magazine*, were bought out by Utlem Publications, which was in turn acquired by Centaur Publications (a publisher of pulp magazines) in 1938, and Centaur Comics was born. The company would only last four years, but most Centaur titles are very collectible today. Important 1930s titles include *Amazing Man Comics* (June 1939), *Amazing Mystery Funnies* (August 1938), *Detective Picture Stories* (December 1936), *Keen Detective Funnies* (July 1938), and *Star Ranger Funnies*.

MARVEL COMICS (TIMELY COMICS)

The major comics publisher Marvel began in late 1939 with *Marvel Comics* #1 (1939, some copies are listed as October, most have November overprinted). This is, after *Action Comics* and *Detective Comics*, the most important comic book of the thirties.

OTHER 1930s PUBLISHERS

United Features: *Tip Top Comics* (begun April 1936)

and *Comics On Parade* (April 1938) both contained reprints of *Tarzan*, *Li'l Abner*, and other United Feature Syndicate newspaper strips; *Single Series* (1938), more reprint comics, with each issue devoted to a single strip, like *Captain and the Kids*, *Li'l Abner*, and *Ella Cinders*.

Fiction House: began in 1938 with *Jumbo*, an oversized comic featuring all-new content; 1930s titles include *Jumbo Comics* (September 1938).

MLJ: this is the company that would become known as Archie Comics by the late forties; only 1930s title was *Blue Ribbon Comics* (November 1939).

Quality Comics: company formed by "Busy" Arnold; 1930s titles include *Feature Funnies* (October 1937), *Feature Comics* (June 1939), and *Smash Comics* (August 1939).

David McKay: strip reprint comics; long-running *Feature Books* (begun in 1936) spotlighted a different comic character each issue. First 25 issues were oversized 9 inch x 12 inch comics, with black and white interiors.

THINGS TO LOOK FOR

Just about any 1930s comic book in halfway decent condition can be valuable, as most comics from this period are considered scarce or rare today. Even copies with missing pages or covers can have significant value. Best bets are DC and Centaur, but anything with superheroes is highly sought-after by collectors.

THINGS TO AVOID

Not much to worry about here, but lower-value comics will be the ones with all newspaper strip reprints. Even some of the Dell titles with heroes are generally less valuable than anything from DC, Fox, or Centaur.

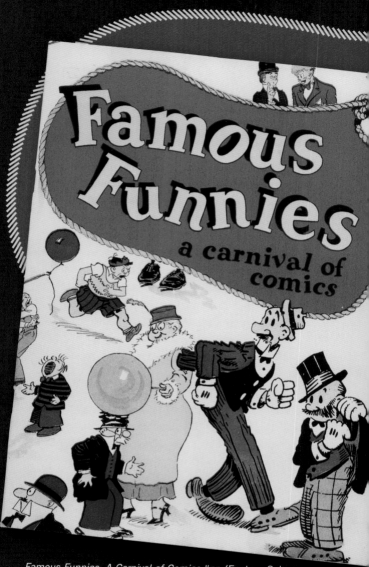

Famous Funnies: A Carnival of Comics #nn (Eastern Color, 1933), CGC NM- 9.2. A copy of the second comic book ever published, this never actually hit newsstands; publisher M. C. Gaines, the "father of the comic book," marketed it to various retailers to use as a promotional giveaway for their customers. At the time, nobody knew if people would actually pay ten cents for one. The content consists of reprints of popular strips of the day, with Mutt and Jeff and others, **$8,365**.

Famous Funnies #1 (Eastern Color, 1934), cover only, front cover from the debut issue, **$209.13**.

Skippy's Own Book of Comics #nn (no publisher, 1934), CGC VF- 7.5. This is widely viewed as the fourth comic book ever produced, published by Max C. Gaines, **$3,170**.

Crackajack Funnies #1 (Dell, 1938), CGC NM/MT. One of Dell's earliest titles, over 20 different strips were represented in this first issue, including Dan Dunn, Don Winslow, Buck Jones, Tom Mix, Myra North, Major Hoople, and others, **$11,950**.

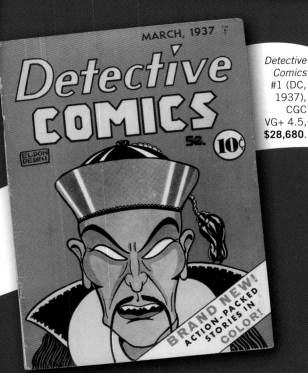

Detective Comics #1 (DC, 1937), CGC VG+ 4.5, **$28,680**.

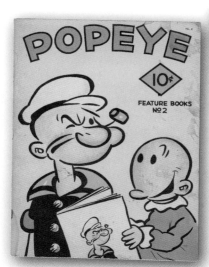

Feature Books *Popeye* #2 (David McKay, 1937), Very Fine. One of the nicest *Popeye* covers featuring Popeye and Swee'pea, **$431.25**.

New Fun Comics #1 (DC, 1935), apparent VG. DC began their comics empire with this initial offering, an oversized anthology of mixed genre material. Unlike other comic books of the day featuring newspaper strip reprints, the contents of *New Fun* were produced especially for this title. It was a revolutionary idea that quickly transformed the fledgling comics industry, and led directly to the publication of such iconic characters as Superman and Batman, **$5,377.50**.

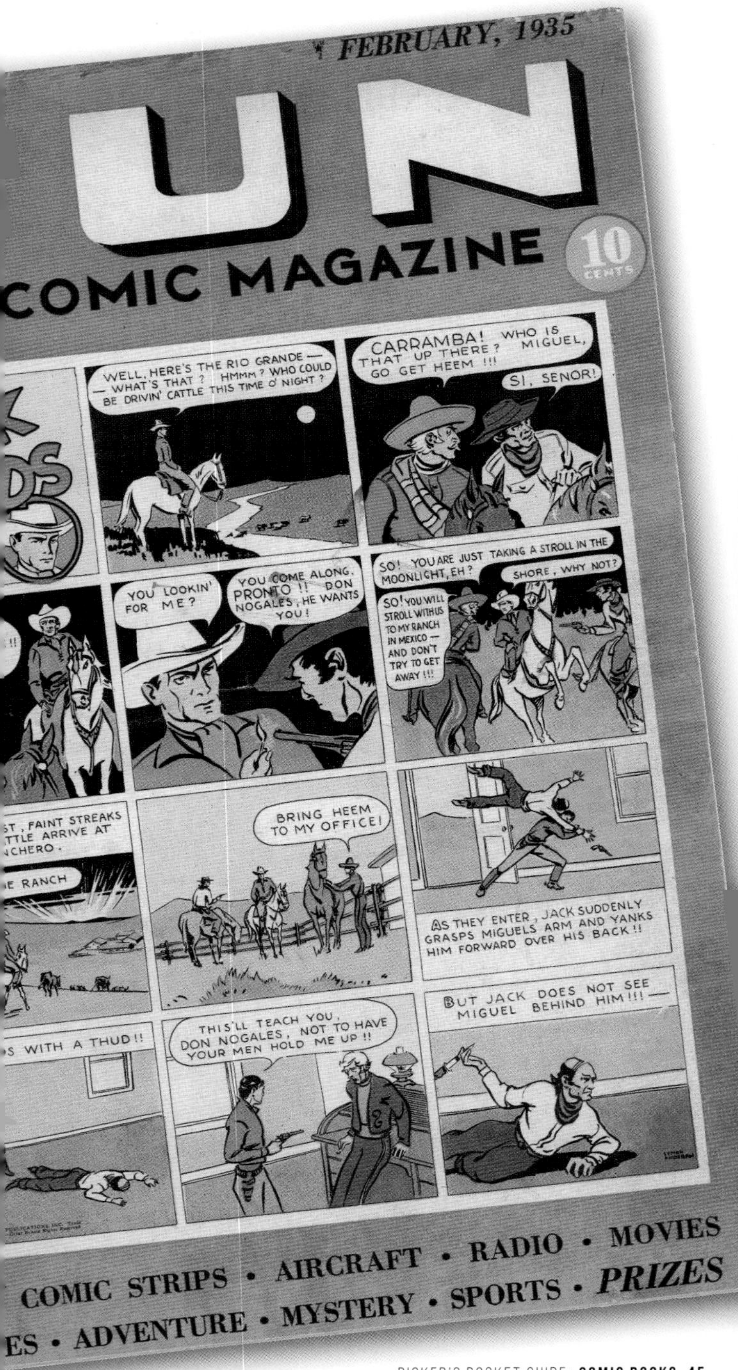
FEBRUARY, 1935
UN
COMIC MAGAZINE
10 CENTS
WELL, HERE'S THE RIO GRANDE — WHAT'S THAT ? HMMM ? WHO COULD BE DRIVIN' CATTLE THIS TIME O' NIGHT ?
CARRAMBA! WHO IS THAT UP THERE ? MIGUEL, GO GET HEEM !!!
SI, SENOR!
YOU LOOKIN' FOR ME ?
YOU COME ALONG, PRONTO !! DON NOGALES, HE WANTS YOU !
SO! YOU ARE JUST TAKING A STROLL IN THE MOONLIGHT, EH ?
SHORE, WHY NOT?
SO! YOU WILL STROLL WITH US TO MY RANCH IN MEXICO — AND DON'T TRY TO GET AWAY !!!
BRING HEEM TO MY OFFICE!
AS THEY ENTER, JACK SUDDENLY GRASPS MIGUELS' ARM AND YANKS HIM FORWARD OVER HIS BACK !!
THIS'LL TEACH YOU, DON NOGALES, NOT TO HAVE YOUR MEN HOLD ME UP !!
BUT JACK DOES NOT SEE MIGUEL BEHIND HIM !!! —
COMIC STRIPS • AIRCRAFT • RADIO • MOVIES
ADVENTURE • MYSTERY • SPORTS • PRIZES

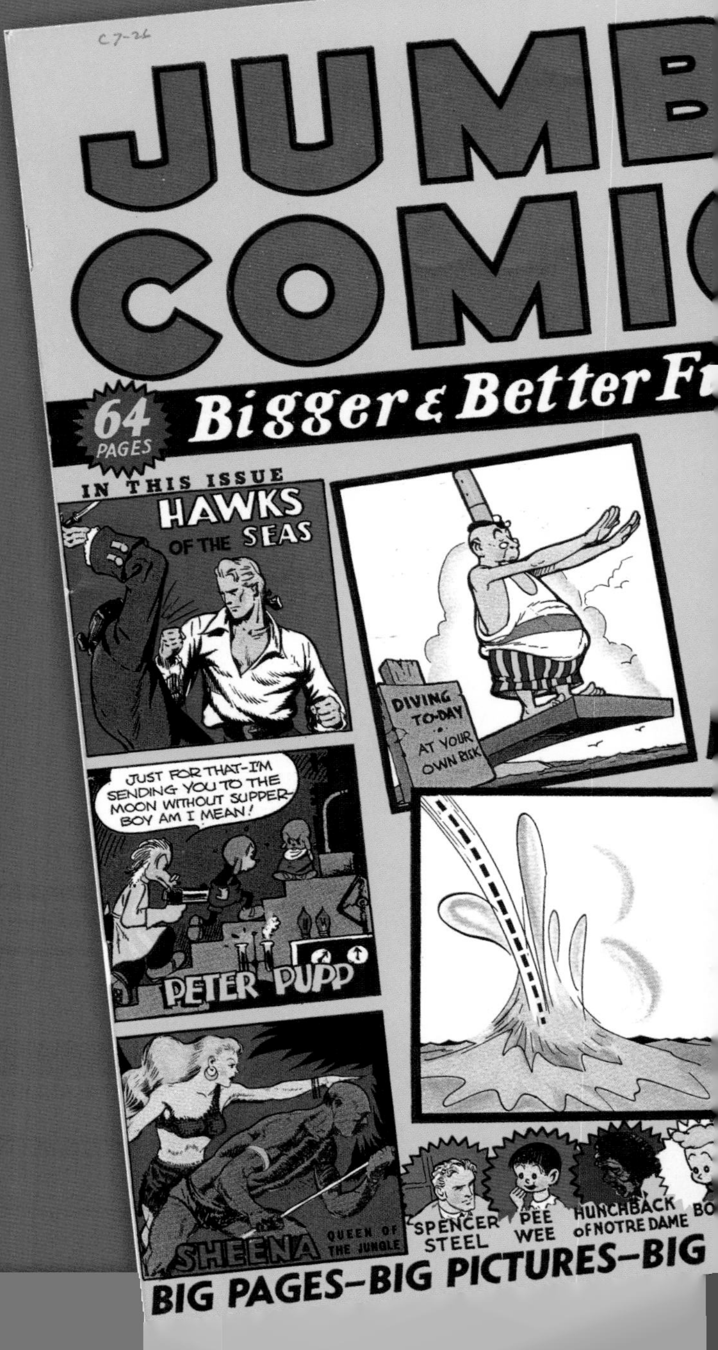

C7-26
JUMB
COMIC
64 PAGES
Bigger & Better Fu
IN THIS ISSUE
HAWKS OF THE SEAS
DIVING TO-DAY
AT YOUR OWN RISK
JUST FOR THAT-I'M SENDING YOU TO THE MOON WITHOUT SUPPER-BOY AM I MEAN!
PETER PUPP
SHEENA QUEEN OF THE JUNGLE
SPENCER STEEL
PEE WEE
HUNCHBACK OF NOTRE DAME
BO
BIG PAGES–BIG PICTURES–BIG

No. 1
SEPT.

nies 10¢

Jumbo Comics #1-8 (Fiction House, 1938-39), Average VF+. These are the huge oversized issues from the early run of the title, with each one measuring 10-1/2" x 14-1/2", **$83,650.**

ALSO... PUZZLE PHUN, JOKES
MODERN PLANES, INSPECTOR
DAYTON, COUNT OF MONTE
CRISTO, WILTON OF THE WEST
AND MANY OTHER FAVORITES
PRIZES — STORIES — FUN

ZX-5

YPE—EASY TO READ

Amazing Mystery Funnies #7 (Centaur, 1939), FN-. Contains the first appearance of the Fantom of the Fair (he plied his trade at the New York World's Fair that was going on at that time), cover art by Paul Gustavson, **$717**.

Four Color (Series One) #1 *Dick Tracy* (Dell, 1939), CGC VF/NM 9.0, **$6,871.25**.

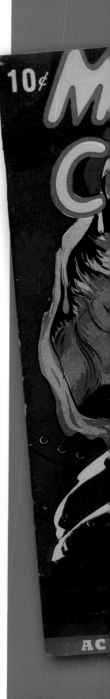

Marvel Comics #1 (Timely, 1939), CGC
VF- 7.5, **$113,525**.

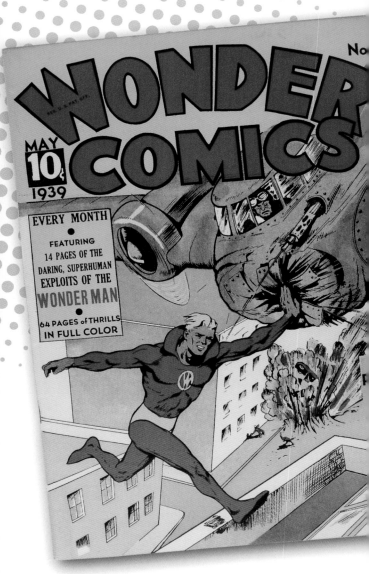

Wonder Comics #1 (Fox, 1939), CGC NM 9.4. The first hero to ride Superman's coat-tails was Wonder Man, who made his debut in this issue. Publisher Victor Fox was immediately slapped with a lawsuit by DC for infringement on their character Superman, causing Fox to withdraw his creation from future issues, **$68,712.50**.

Blue Ribbon Comics #1 (MLJ, 1939), CGC NM 9.4. The the first comic published by MLJ (later known as Archie Publications), it features the first appearances of Dan Hastings, Richy the Amazing Boy, and Rang-A-Tang the Wonder Dog. Cover attributed to Norman Danberg; Golden Age great Jack Cole contributed interior art, **$4,780**.

Smash Comics #1 (Quality, 1939), CGC VF/NM 9.0. The great Will Eisner drew a story for this issue, "Espionage"; also of note are the first appearances of Hooded Justice, Chic Carter, and Wings Wendall, **$2,990**.

Batman #1 (DC, 1940), CGC NM- 9.2. This issue has the first appearances of both the Joker and Catwoman, two of the very few villains to have "household name" status, and the cover art by Bob Kane and Jerry Robinson is one of the most recognizable of all comic book covers, **$567,625**.

CHAPTER 3

The 1940s

THE GOLDEN AGE

The heart of the "Golden Age of Comics" occurred in the 1940s, a time that saw tremendous growth in terms of titles published, characters, and new publishers entering the field. As Superman and Batman grew more popular, more publishers jumped in, and the circulation for an average comic book rose to incredible numbers. It wasn't uncommon for a single issue of a popular comic title to sell a million or more copies during this time.

Back in the old days of comic fandom, circa 1960-75, the "true" Golden Age was considered to be 1940-43. Comics were still 64 pages, plus covers, with every page in full, vibrant color. World War II paper rationing began in earnest in 1943, gutting the content down to 32 pages, plus covers; in fact, paper was in such short supply during 1944 and '45 that half-sheets were used. Many an unknowing fan back in the '60s and '70s would notice what appeared to be a page or two neatly cut out, but with no impact on content – this is because scraps of paper were being used to print a two-sided page (rather than a typical four-page leaf), leaving a small stub visible elsewhere within the comic book.

By the end of the war, paper restrictions were eased, and even more publishers tried their hand at producing comic books of all types. There were so many publishers in the 1940s that we can't list them all, but here's a run-down on the most important producers of comics during this time:

DC/ALL-AMERICAN

DC led the way with their flagship titles *Action Comics* and *Detective Comics*, plus other anthology-style titles like *More Fun Comics*, *Sensation Comics*, and *All-American Comics*. All-American was basically a stand-alone company that worked closely with National Periodicals, the parent company of DC. Their main characters were the Flash, Green Lantern, the Atom, Hawkman, and Wonder Woman. At first, all issues carried the DC logo on the covers, but early in 1945, they started using a new "AA" logo. However, by 1946, National had bought All-American Publications out, and the familiar DC bullet logo once again appeared on all the former AA titles.

IMPORTANT DC TITLES IN THE 1940s:

- *Action Comics* (starring Superman)
- *Adventure Comics* (a number of different features resided here, most notably the Sandman and Sandy)
- *All-American Comics* (home to the Green Lantern and others)
- *All Star Comics* (home to the Justice Society of America, featuring an ever-changing roster of heroes that included Flash, Green Lantern, Wonder Woman, Atom, Hawkman, the Sandman, Dr. Fate, Hourman, and several others)
- *Batman*
- *Big All-American Comic Book* (a 132-page one-shot comic from 1944)
- *Boy Comandos*
- *Detective Comics* (home to Batman)

1. **ALL-AMERICAN COMICS #16**
2. **BATMAN #1**
3. **CAPTAIN AMERICA COMICS #1**
   (FIRST APPEARANCE OF CAPTAIN AMERICA)
4. **FLASH COMICS #1**
   (FIRST APPEARANCE OF THE FLASH)
5. **PEP COMICS #22**
   (FIRST APPEARANCE OF ARCHIE)
6. **MORE FUN COMICS #52**
   (FIRST APPEARANCE OF THE SPECTRE)
7. **WHIZ COMICS #2 (#1)**
   (FIRST APPEARANCE OF CAPTAIN MARVEL)
8. **ARCHIE COMICS #1**
9. **ALL STAR COMICS #3**
10. **ALL STAR COMICS #8**

Flash Comics #1
Mile High pedigree
(DC, 1940), CGC
NM+ 9.6. One of
the most important
comic books of any
age, *Flash Comics*
#1 features the
origins and first
appearances of the
Flash, Hawkman,
Shiera Sanders,
the Whip, and
Johnny Thunder.
Sheldon Moldoff
contributed cover
and interior art,
$273,125.

- *Flash Comics* (co-starring Hawkman and Hawkgirl)
- *Leading Comics* (featuring a second heroic team, the Seven Soldiers of Victory, which included Green Arrow and Speedy, Johnny Quick, Vigilante, Shining Knight, and the Star-Spangled Kid & Stripesy)
- *New York World's Fair Comics* – 1940 edition
- *Sensation Comics* (Wonder Woman's flagship title)
- *Star-Spangled Comics*
- *Superman*
- *Superboy* (first introduced in *More Fun #101*, before moving to Adventure Comics and his own title)
- *Wonder Woman* (first introduced in *All Star Comics* #8)
- *World's Best Comics* (100-page comic; becomes *World's Finest Comics* with issue #2)

DC also published a number of humor titles in the forties: *All Funny Comics, Animal Antics, Mutt and Jeff,* and *Real Screen Comics*; in the post-war years, several titles that once featured superhero stories switched to all humor: *Comic Cavalcade, Leading Comics,* and (briefly) *More Fun*.

TIMELY COMICS

The second most important comics publisher of the 1940s, this is the company that became Atlas Comics in the 1950s and Marvel Comics in the 1960s. Timely produced scads of titles, many with obscure superheroes that lasted only an issue or two before vanishing completely. The most enduring characters are Captain America, Sub-Mariner, and the Human Torch. Timely comics are highly sought after by modern collectors, and are generally harder to find than other major publishers of the era. Here are some of the most important titles to look for:

- *All Select Comics* (1943-45, featured the "big three," Captain America, Sub-Mariner, and Human Torch)
- *All Winners Comics* (1941-46, with a Volume Two issue in 1948, features the All-Winners Squad with Captain America and other characters)
- *Captain America Comics* (first issue dated March

Daring Mystery Comics #6 (Timely, 1940), CGC
VF/NM 9.0. The Simon and Kirby team put their
stamp on this issue, drawing the cover and writing
and illustrating two stories, **$4,929.38**.

1941; first ten-issue feature art by the team of Joe Simon and Jack Kirby, and are some of the most collectible comics of all time)

- *Daring Mystery Comics* (1940-42, had a revolving cast of "second banana" heroes like The Whizzer, Marvel Boy, The Fin, The Fiery Mask, The Blue Diamond, The Purple Mask, The Thunderer, and many more)
- *Human Torch Comics* (first issue listed as #2; ran from 1940 to '49)
- *Kid Komics* (ten-issue anthology series running from 1943-'46, starring Captain Wonder, the Young Allies, The Vision, The Destroyer, and others)
- *Marvel Mystery Comics* (the flagship title, starring Human Torch and Sub-Mariner, often battling each other in early issues)
- *Mystic Comics* (two separate anthology series; Volume 1 ran from 1940-42, while Volume 2 ran from 1944-45; characters included Blazing Skull, Destroyer, Flexo the Rubber Man , Black Widow, Angel, Human Torch, and Young Allies)
- *Red Raven Comics* (rare one-shot title from 1940, highly sought-after)
- *Sub-Mariner Comics* (ran for 42 issues, beginning in 1941)
- *Sun Girl* (ran for only three issues in 1948)
- *Two-Gun Kid* (Western comic that ran throughout the '40s, '50s, '60s, and into the '70s; 1940s run was from 1948-49)
- *U.S.A. Comics* (17-issue heroic anthology, featuring Captain America, The Defender, Whizzer, Rockman, Captain Terror, and others)
- *Young Allies* (kid team led by Captain America's sidekick, Bucky, and Human Torch's boy companion, Toro; ran for 20 issues from 1941 to '46)

A partial list of other 1940s Timely titles included *Comedy Comics, Joker Comics, Terrytoons Comics,*

Mighty Mouse, All Surprise Comics, Super Rabbit Comics, Funny Frolics, Funny Tunes, Millie the Model, Tessie the Typist, Nellie the Nurse (all humor-related titles) *Powerhouse Pepper* (five-issue series featuring art by Basil Wolverton, very collectible), *Namora (*a Sub-Mariner spin-off), and *Venus*. While humor and Western titles are not as collectible as the superheroes, all Timely comics in decent shape are worth money.

One very collectible aspect of Timely issues during World War II were patriotic covers featuring superheroes battling German and Japanese soldiers, occasionally starring Hitler, Tojo, and Mussolini. Most of the covers were drawn by Alex Schomburg, and are highly sought-after.

FAWCETT PUBLICATIONS

Fawcett's Captain Marvel was for a time the biggest-selling comic book hero of the 1940s, often outselling Superman, Batman, and Captain America. These comics were geared toward a slightly younger audience, and were a little more "cartoony" in appearance. The character was originally modeled after movie star Fred MacMurray, and soon had an entire family of similar characters. Known lovingly as the Big Red Cheese, Captain Marvel's popularity brought about a lawsuit from DC/National, claiming copyright infringement due to the similar nature of Captain Marvel's powers to

Nickel Comics #1 (Fawcett, 1940) CGC VF- 7.5 O. Bulletman made his first appearance in this issue, which also tells the character's origin story (he not only invents a serum that gives him superpowers, but also comes up with his gravity-defying helmet), **$1,553.50**.

Superman. The suit was not settled until the 1950s.

Some important Fawcett titles:

- *Bulletman*
- *Captain Marvel Adventures*
- *Captain Marvel Jr.*
- *Captain Midnight*
- *The Marvel Family*
- *Mary Marvel Comics*
- *Master Comics*
- *Minute Man*
- *Nickel Comics* (one of the very few five-cent comics produced; had half the number of pages as the ten centers)
- *Slam Bang Comics*
- *Whiz Comics* (the flagship title, which introduced Captain Marvel in 1940 with issue #2–there was no #1)
- *Wow Comics*

In addition to these superhero titles, Fawcett also published *Don Winslow of the Navy, Fawcett's Funny Animals, Gabby Hayes Western, Hopalong Cassidy, Hoppy the Marvel Bunny* (a super-powered rabbit, part of the Marvel Family), *Lash Larue Western, Monte Hale Western, Nyoka the Jungle Girl, Rocky Lane Western, Sweethearts*, and *Tom Mix Western*. These are collectible when in better than average condition, but not particularly rare or valuable.

FICTION HOUSE

Pulp magazine producer, comic line anchored by flagship title *Jumbo Comics*; other titles included:

- *Fight Comics*
- *Jungle Comics* (featuring Sheena, Queen of the Jungle)
- *Ka'a'nga, Jungle King*
- *Planet Comics* (influential science-fiction title, begun in 1940)
- *Rangers Comics*
- *Wings Comics*

Planet Comics #24 (Fiction House, 1943), CGC NM- 9.2. The cover, featuring bird-riding warrior maidens, is by Dan Zolnerowich, and the interior art is by Graham Ingels, Lee Elias, and George Tuska. **$2,629**

FOX FEATURE SYNDICATE/FOX PUBLICATIONS/FOX COMICS

Fox produced a lesser-quality line of comics, but not without some very collectible titles, especially the pre-1943 issues. Fox was known for having great covers and less-than-great interior art, but there were plenty of exceptions. Here are some of the most important Fox titles:

- *All Top Comics*
- *Big Three*
- *Blue Beetle*
- *Crimes By Women* (1948-50)
- *Dagar, Desert Hawk*
- *Fantastic Comics* (ran for 23 issues, beginning in 1941)
- *The Green Mask* (17 issues, 1940-46)
- *Jo-Jo Comics* and *Jo-Jo Jungle King* (1946-49 jungle hero)
- *Junior Comics* (#9-16 beginning in 1946; "Archie" style teen humor with "Good Girl" art by Al Feldstein, quite collectible)
- *Mystery Men Comics* (31 issues, ran until 1942)
- *Phantom Lady* (very collectible "Good Girl" art title, 1947-49)
- *Rex Dexter of Mars* (one issue, 1940)
- *Rocket Kelly*
- *Rulah, Jungle Goddess* (1948-49 "Good Girl" jungle hero)
- *Samson* (six issues, 1940-41)
- *Science Comics* (eight issues from 1940, many with Lou Fine art on the covers)
- *Sunny, America's Sweetheart* (similar to *Junior Comics*; 1947-48)
- *V...- Comics* (two issues, 1942)
- *Weird Comics* (twenty issues, 1940-42)
- *Women Outlaws*
- *Wonder Comics* (changes to *Wonderworld Comics* with #3; 33 issues running through 1942)
- *Zoot Comics*

Many other titles were produced by this publisher, including Westerns, Funny Animal, Crime, Romance, Jungle, etc. Production became increasingly lower-quality, especially after WWII. These comics were printed on poor paper, and are rarely found in like-new condition.

QUALITY COMICS

Quality produced some of the best art in the early 1940s, with such artists as Lou Fine, Reed Crandall, Will Eisner, and Jack Cole contributing fantastic story illustration. The company was later acquired by DC. Here are the more important titles of the 1940s:

Hit Comics #10 (Quality, 1941), GD. Cover by Lou Fine; art by Reed Crandall, his first comic book work, **$274.85**.

- *Blackhawk*
- *Crack Comics*
- *Doll Man*
- *Feature Comics*
- *Hit Comics*
- *Kid Eternity*
- *Lady Luck*
- *Military Comics* (featuring Blackhawk; becomes *Modern Comics* with issue #44)
- *National Comics* (starring a hero named Uncle Sam)
- *Plastic Man* (by Jack Cole)
- *Police Comics* (introduced Plastic Man)
- *Smash Comics*
- *The Spirit* (reprinted Will Eisner's iconic masked crime fighter, from newspaper comic sections)
- *Torchy* ("Good Girl" title began in 1948; ran for six issues into 1950)
- *Uncle Sam Quarterly*

Many other titles, mostly humor related, with a few romance and crime titles near the end of the decade.

Archie Comics #1 (MLJ, 1942), CGC VF+ 8.5, **$167,300**.

MLJ/ARCHIE

MLJ began with heroic titles featuring characters like The Shield, Hangman, Steel Sterling, Black Hood, and The Wizard, before a certain red-headed teenager named Archie Andrews made his first appearance in 1942. Here are the most important MLJ titles:

- *Black Hood*
- *Blue Ribbon Comics*
- *Hangman Comics*
- *Jackpot Comics*
- *Pep Comics* (introduces Archie with issue #22)
- *Shield-Wizard Comics*
- *Top-Notch Comics*
- *Zip Comics*

Most Archie-related titles from the 1940s are quite collectible, especially in better-than-average condition.

OTHER 1940S COMIC PUBLISHERS

There were so many producers of comics in the 1940s that it would fill the book to list every one, so here are some highlights:

- Ace Comics (*Sure-Fire Comics, Super-Mystery Comics, Lightning, Four Favorites, Banner Comics, Our Flag*)
- Better/Nedor/Standard (titles like *Black Terror, Fighting Yank, Thrilling, Exciting* featuring The Black Terror, *Doc Strange* [not the later Marvel Comics character], *Captain Future*
- Centaur (*Amazing Adventure Funnies, Amazing Man Comics, Fantoman, Stars and Stripes, Super Spy, Keen Detective Funnies* – most Centaur titles are difficult to find and are highly collectible)
- Charlton Comics (a few 1940s titles like *Yellowjacket*; became more prolific in the 1950s-60s)
- Chesler (*Punch Comics, Yankee Comics, Dynamic Comics, Scoop Comics*)
- Columbia Comics (*Big Shot, The Face, Skyman, Sparky Watts*)

- Dell Comics (published mostly humor and newspaper strip reprints, plus a number of comics based on strips like *Flash Gordon*. Best known today for their line of Disney titles)
- Eastern/Famous Funnies (*Heroic Comics*)
- Gilberton (*Classic Comics/Classics Illustrated*)
- Great Comics Publications
- Harvey Comics (although better known for their line of children's humor titles, Harvey specialized in heroic titles during the 1940s, such as *All-New Comics, Black Cat, Champion/Champ Comics, Shock Comics,* and *Speed Comics*)
- Hillman (*Miracle Comics, Clue Comics, Air Fighters, Air Boy, Victory Comics, Rocket Comics*)
- Holyoke (*Crash Comics, Catman Comics, Captain Aero, Captain Fearless, Cyclone Comics, Whirlwind Comics*)
- Hyper Publications (*Hyper-Mystery Comics*)
- Lev Gleason (*Silver Streak, Daredevil Comics* [first issue was titled *Daredevil Battles Hitler*, a true WWII classic], *Boy Comics, Crime Does Not Pay* [first big-selling Crime title, with many imitators; first big new trend after WWII in comic books)
- Novelty/Funnies Inc. (*Target Comics, Blue Bolt, Four Most*)
- Prize (*Prize Comics*)
- Street and Smith (Pulp magazine producer; comic titles include *The Shadow, Doc Savage Comics, Red Dragon Comics, Super Magician Comics, Super Magic Comics*)
- United Features (*O.K. Comics, Sparkman, Sparkler Comics*)

WHAT TO LOOK FOR

Just about any 1940s comic in above average condition can be valuable. Be on the lookout for comics with great covers, or "eye appeal"; bondage covers; WWII-related; "Good Girl"/"Headlights" (busty women); most

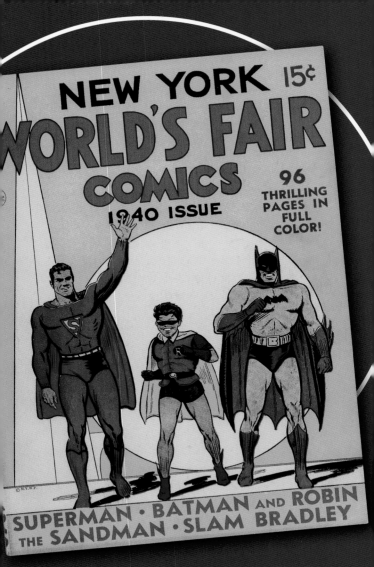

New York World's Fair Comics (DC, 1940), CGC VF 8.0. This early DC annual-sized issue is notable for having Batman, Robin, and Superman all appear together for the first time, as the World's Finest team wave to the World's Fair crowd on this Jack Burnley cover (his first). It's also very early in young Robin's career, coming about two months after his debut in *Detective Comics* #38. Hourman, the Sandman, Johnny Thunderbolt, Zatara, and Slam Bradley are also featured, **$7,767**.

if not all superheroes: lurid Crime and Romance covers.

The "cool factor" is important – how cool-looking is the cover? Collectors like certain covers with American flags, Christmas themes, nice Sports themes, and "infinity" covers, where the character appears to be holding a copy of the same comic, and the detail includes covers-within-covers, getting smaller and smaller.

Among Disney comics, the best titles were part of Dell's *Four Color* one-shot line, featuring Donald Duck (with book-length stories and art by Carl Barks, who did not sign his work, but with an obvious quality to his art – look for the little "pie-slice" highlights in the Duck's eyes). Some early Mickey Mouse, like *Four Color* #16 (Mickey Mouse vs the Phantom Blot) and *Four Color* #79 ("Riddle of the Red Hat" by Carl Barks) are popular with collectors.

WHAT TO AVOID

Be careful of *Classic Comics* and *Classics Illustrated*, as many of their issues were reprinted over and over again; first edition issues usually have an ad for the next issue on the back cover or inside front cover. Be sure to check Overstreet's *Classic Illustrated* listings. I've fielded hundreds if not thousands of calls from people who find a stack of old *Classics* in their attics; these types of comic books were saved when others were tossed out, and are far more common than most from the era.

Most Westerns like *Roy Rogers* and *Gene Autry* were highly popular with collectors for many years, but in more recent years they've faded quite a bit in desirability, as old collectors die out or quit actively collecting, and there seems to be little interest in younger collectors.

Early War comics are not that popular, unless the cover is exceptional. Reality-based titles like *True Comics* have little demand, as do most obscure funny animal titles. Condition is the key here – if the book looks close to brand-new/unread, it might have some real value, but average used copies tend to bring very little in today's market.

All-American Comics #16 (DC, 1940), CGC VF 8.0. The first appearance of Green Lantern is one of the top five comic issues in the hobby. The character was created by Martin Nodell, and the cover art for the first issue was by Sheldon Moldoff, **$203,150.**

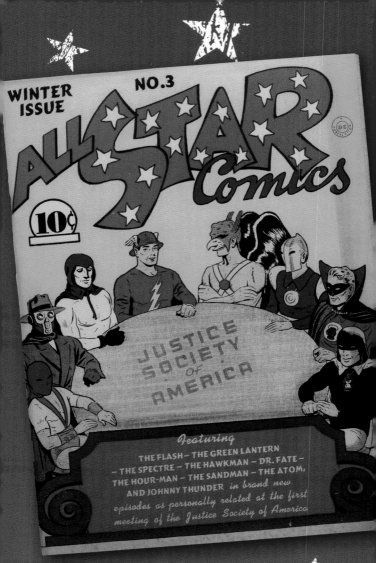

All Star Comics #3 (DC, 1940), CGC VF+ 8.5. Features first appearance of Justice Society of America, the first superhero group, **$49,293.75**.

All Star Comics #8 (DC, 1942), CGC VF 8.0. One of the most important issues in DC's history has the origin and first appearance of Wonder Woman by H. G. Peter, **$56,762.50**.

Pep Comics #22 (MLJ, 1941), CGC FN/VF 7.0. While the Shield, Dusty, and the Hangman got the cover spot, the real star doesn't show until a six-page story, tucked away in the second half of the comic book. Archie Andrews makes his first appearance, along with his pals Jughead and Betty (Veronica comes a little later). Archie has been "America's Teenager" for so many years, it's hard to imagine him happening before World War II, but this issue was cover dated December 1941, and came out a few weeks before Pearl Harbor was attacked, **$143,400**.

Archie debuts!

More Fun Comics #52 (DC, 1940), CGC NM- 9.2. This comic is so sought-after that any unrestored copy in even decent condition brings a hefty sum at auction. What earned the book a spot among the most valuable comics is the origin and first appearance of the Spectre, which brought a whole new direction to the anthology title that was DC's first comic book series. The Spectre tale was written by the co-creator of one of those wondermen, Jerry Siegel, and drawn by Bernard Baily, **$119,500**.

Speed Comics #18 Mile High pedigree (Harvey, 1942), VF/NM. This bondage cover by Simon and Kirby is quite significant when you consider that the first horror comic appeared in 1943 or 1947 depending on your opinion, **$2,390.**

Captain America Comics #2 (Timely, 1941), CGC NM 9.4. This is the second appearance of Captain America, but the first appearance of the Captain costume most are familiar with, including his trademark round shield. The classic cover is by the great Joe Simon. As with issue #1, Adolf Hitler himself was the featured cover villain, though this was before the United States had entered World War II, **$113,525.**

Whiz Comics #2 (#1) (Fawcett, 1940), CGC GD/VG 3.0. This is one of the ten most valuable comic books, due to the origin and first appearance of Captain Marvel. It's also the debut of baddie Dr. Sivana and a host of other characters including Spy Smasher and Ibis the Invincible, **$7,170.**

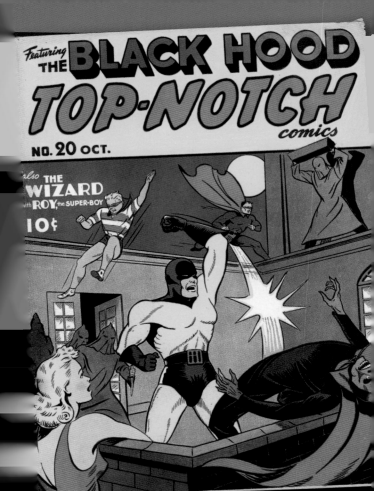

Top-Notch Comics #20 (MLJ, 1941), apparent VG. Al Camy cover, The Black Hood, the Wizard, Roy the Super-Boy, the Firefly, Kardak, and Bob Phantom appear, **$48**.

Cat-Man Comics #3 (Holyoke Publications, 1941), GD. Classic Hitler, Stalin, and Mussolini cover by Charles Quinlan, who handled interior art as well, **$299**.

Marvel Mystery Comics #40 (Timely, 1943), CGC VF/NM 9.0.
Classic cover art by Alex Schomburg, **$21,510**.

Phantom Lady #13 (Fox Features Syndicate, 1947), VG+. First issue of the title featuring Phantom Lady by Matt Baker; there is also a Blue Beetle story, **$1,015.75**.

Showcase #4 *The Flash* (DC, 1956), CGC VF/NM 9.0. The most valuable Silver Age DC issue, this book introduced a new version of the Flash at a time when superheroes were all but dead. Only Superman, Batman, and Wonder Woman had their own DC titles at the time, and Atlas/Marvel wasn't publishing a single costumed crusader. The new Flash, Barry Allen, had a sleek look unlike any costume seen in the Golden Age, and the art style was exciting and new, courtesy of artist Carmine Infantino, **$38,837.50**.

The 1950s

After the end of World War II, most superhero comics lost their appeal; only the "strongest" of them survived the end of the era and into the 1950s, like Batman, Superman, Wonder Woman, and Captain Marvel. The heroic comics were soon replaced by Crime titles, which had become popular in the late 1940s. The bloodier and more violent the cover, the better it sold, and that paved the way to the next big wave – Horror. Most publishers that survived into the '50s turned to Horror, with each company attempting to "out-gross" the other, resulting in incredibly lurid covers. Eventually, a backlash from concerned parents, teachers, and doctors began to publicly attack these horrific comic books, insisting that young minds could not handle such violence without traumatic damage to their thinking. Comic books would go on to be decried by many authorities and church groups as a leading cause of juvenile delinquency, which was a growing problem at the time. As a result, a Comics Code Authority was set up to monitor the content, effectively ending the reign of violent Crime and Horror titles.

EC COMICS

Educational Comics began as an offshoot of DC, and their initial output would be titles like *Picture Stories from the Bible*. Under publisher William E. Gaines, who inherited the company after his father, Max Gaines, died in a boating accident, the newly rechristened Entertaining Comics tried a number of different Crime, Funny Animal,

Humor, Western, and Romance titles, none of which were big sellers. In 1950, the focus shifted to Horror, with the publication of *The Crypt of Horror*. After three issues, the name was changed to *Tales from the Crypt*, and was soon joined by *The Vault of Horror* and *Haunt of Fear*. All were huge sellers. The key to EC's success was the combination of well-crafted stories (usually with a "twist" ending) and top-of-the-line art by Wally Wood, Al Feldstein, Johnny Craig, Graham Ingels, Joe Orlando, and others.

As the Horror titles continued to sell well, the EC line soon expanded to include Science Fiction (*Weird Science* and *Weird Fantasy*), War (the excellent *Two-Fisted Tales* and *Frontline Combat*, written and sometimes drawn by Harvey Kurtzman); plus Crime and Suspense titles with twist endings (*Crime SuspenStories* and *Shock SuspenStories*). The line expanded even further when Gaines gave Kurtzman a humor title, which far outlived all the other ECs: *MAD*.

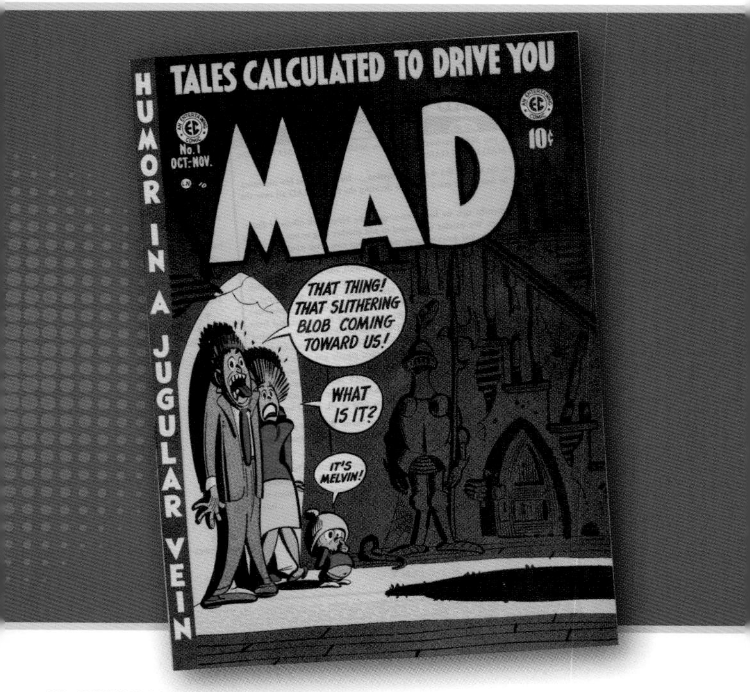
TALES CALCULATED TO DRIVE YOU
MAD
HUMOR IN A JUGULAR VEIN
No. 1
OCT-NOV.
10¢
THAT THING! THAT SLITHERING BLOB COMING TOWARD US!
WHAT IS IT?
IT'S MELVIN!

CHAPTER 4

MAD began as a regular ten-cent comic book with satire as its primary focus – the first real comic book of its kind. The first few issues had generic spoofs, but soon found gold by lampooning newspaper comics, movies, and more. Led by artist/writer Harvey Kurtzman (who would soon curtail his drawing to concentrate on writing), artists like Wally Wood, Bill Elder (now better known as Will Elder), John Severin, Jack Davis, and a few others turned the world of humor comics upside down. The *MAD* comic book lasted 23 issues before it was converted into a magazine. All the comic book issues are valuable in average used condition or better.

EC eventually gave up publishing everything except the magazine version of *MAD* when the Comics Code came into effect in 1954, and newsdealers began refusing to carry any of the company's line, due to concerns over their line of Horror titles. For many years, any EC was hotly collected, but after a series of reprint issues in

1950s COMICS

TOP 10

1. *SHOWCASE* #4 (THE FLASH)
2. *THE FLASH* #105
3. *SHOWCASE* #9 (LOIS LANE)
4. *VAULT OF HORROR* #12
5. *JOURNEY INTO MYSTERY* #1
6. *TALES OF TERROR ANNUAL* #1
7. *MAD* #1
8. *STRANGE TALES* #1
9. *CRYPT OF TERROR* #17
10. *HAUNT OF FEAR* #15

MAD #1 (EC, 1952), CGC NM/MT 9.8. Few titles have managed to last as long as Harvey Kurtzman's brain-child, which is still going strong today. Kurtzman drew the cover to this seminal issue, **$32,200**.

the 1980s appeared, demand became a little less; these books, particularly those in exceptional condition, continue to be popular with collectors.

OTHER 1950S TRENDS

DC continued to publish *Action Comics, Adventure Comics, Detective Comics, Sensation Comics, World's Finest Comics*, and solo titles for *Batman, Superman, Superboy*, and *Wonder Woman* throughout the 1950s. The company also produced Science Fiction titles (*Mystery in Space, Strange Adventures, My Greatest Adventure*), Crimefighters (*Big Town, Gangbusters, Mr. District Attorney*), Mystery (*House of Mystery, House of Secrets*), Westerns (*All-Star Western, Western Comics, Dale Evans Comics, Tomahawk*) War (*Our Army At War* starring Sgt. Rock of Easy Company; *G.I. Combat, All-American Men of War, Star Spangled War Stories*), and a number of Teen and Humor titles (*Leave it to Binky, A Date With Judy, The Fox and Crow, Sugar and Spike, Adventures of Bob Hope*, and many others). DC comics from the Korean War years (1950-53), have been known to be scarce. Here are a few of the harder DC titles to find from this era:

BEST PICKER FIND

Alex Miller, Heritage Auctions: It had to be the *Action Comics* #1 in the Prospect Mountain Collection. Anytime I see a list with *Action 1* on it, I presume it's a fake. He had 27 big boxes in a room and I removed a stack of books from one the boxes and behold! There was the Holy Grail!

- *Danger Trail*
- *Phantom Stranger* (the six-issue series from 1952-53)
- *It's Game Time*
- *Sensation Mystery*

The most important event for DC in the 1950s began with a successful revival of The Flash, in *Showcase #4* (Sept.-Oct. 1956). This updated hero was soon followed by the return of Green Lantern, in *Showcase #22* (Sept.-Oct. 1959). *Showcase* also introduced The Challengers of the Unknown, Space Ranger, and Adam Strange, all of whom would appear throughout the 1960s.

The Superman family was expanded by creating titles for incidental characters Jimmy Olsen (*Superman's Pal Jimmy Olsen*, 1954) and Lois Lane (*Superman's Girl Friend Lois Lane*, 1958).

MARVEL/ATLAS COMICS

Marvel's 1950s output, released under the Atlas imprint, shows a once vibrant company floundering. Main hero Captain America faded after *Captain America Comics* #75 (Feb. 1950), after which the title switched to Horror (*Captain America's Weird Tales*). Focus shifted to just about every other genre possible: Horror, Western, Funny Animal, Teen Humor, Adventure, Crime, War, Jungle, Romance, and more. The heroes made a brief comeback in 1953 with *Young Men* #24, starring The Human Torch, Sub-Mariner, and Captain America, with the heroes even getting their own titles back, but it was all short-lived. The final years of the 1950s were primarily devoted to War, Mystery, and Humor.

Selected 1950s Atlas titles include:
- *Adventure into Mystery*
- *Adventures into Terror*
- *Amazing Detective Cases*
- *Astonishing*
- *Battle*
- *Battle Action*

- *Battleground*
- *Battlefront*
- *Black Knight*
- *Captain America Comics* (issues #76-78)
- *Crazy*
- *The Human Torch* (issues #36-38)
- *Journey into Mystery*
- *Journey into Unknown Worlds*
- *Jungle Action*
- *Jungle Tales/Jann of the Jungle*
- *Lorna, the Jungle Queen/Lorna, the Jungle Girl*
- *Man Comics*
- *Marines in Battle*
- *Marvel Boy* (two issues in 1950-51)
- *Marvel Tales*
- *Menace*
- *Men's Adventure*
- *Miss America*
- *Mystic* (the third series, devoted to Horror and Supernatural stories)
- *The Outlaw Kid*
- *Rawhide Kid*
- *Riot*
- *Spellbound*
- *Spy Fighters*
- *Strange Stories of Suspense*
- *Strange Tales*
- *Strange Tales of the Unusual*
- *Strange Worlds*
- *Sub-Mariner* (issues #33-42)
- *Suspense*
- *Tales of Suspense*
- *Tales to Astonish*
- *Venus*
- *Western Kid*
- *Wild*
- *World of Fantasy*

- *World of Mystery*
- *World of Suspense*
- *Young Men*

OTHER MAJOR 1950S PUBLISHERS

- Ajax/Farrell, aka Farrell Group (*Fantastic Fears, Haunted Thrills, Phantom Lady, Strange Fantasy, Voodoo*)
- Avon (*Attack on Planet Mars, Eerie, Flying Saucers, For a Night of Love, The Mask of Fu Manchu, Night of Mystery, Out of This World, Prison Break, Rocket to the Moon, Slave Girl Comics, Space Comics, Space Detective, Strange Worlds, Witchcraft*)
- American Comics Group (*Adventures into the Unknown, Forbidden Worlds, Out of the Night, Skeleton Hand, Unknown Worlds*)
- Dell (various *Four Color* Comics issues, *Marge's Little Lulu, Tarzan, Uncle Scrooge*)
- Fawcett (Captain Marvel titles including *The Marvel Family*)
- Fox (*Crimes Incorporated, Famous Crimes, Inside Crime*)
- Gilberton (*Classics Illustrated, The World Around Us*)

Out of This World #1 (Avon, 1950), CGC FN. Origin and first appearance of Crom the Barbarian, robot cover by Gene Fawcette, art by Fawcette, John Giunta, and Joe Kubert, **$448.13**.

- Harvey (*Black Cat Mystery, Chamber of Chills, Witches Tales*, various Humor comics like *Casper the Friendly Ghost* and *Little Audrey*)
- Hillman (*Crime Must Stop, Monster Crime Comics, Top Secret*, continuation of *Air Boy*)
- Quality (Continuation of *Blackhawk, Doll Man*, and *Plastic Man; Buccaneers, Candy, Crack Western, Exploits of Daniel Boone, G. I. Combat, Ken Shannon, Robin Hood Tales, Web of Evil*. Company bought out by DC, who continued some titles)
- Prize (*Black Magic, Fighting American, Headline Comics, Justice Traps the Guilty, Strange World of Your Dreams, Young Love, Young Romance* (last two titles continued by DC)
- Standard (*Adventures into Darkness, Best Romance, Crime Files, Exciting War, Fantastic Worlds, Jet Fighters, Joe Yank, Lost Worlds, Out of the Shadows, Thrilling Romances*)
- Star Publications (notable for covers by artist L. B. Cole; titles include *All-Famous Police Cases, Ghostly Weird Stories, Frisky Animals, Popular Teen-Agers, Shocking Mystery Cases*)
- St. John (*1,000,000 Years Ago* [aka *Tor*], *Approved Comics, Atom-Age Combat, Authentic Police Cases, Canteen Kate, House of Terror* [3-D one-shot], *Strange Terrors, Weird Horrors, Whack, Zip-Jet*)
- Ziff Davis (Many titles with beautiful painted covers; titles include *Amazing Adventures, Baseball Thrills, Cloak and Dagger, Crusaders from Mars, Eerie Adventures, Football Thrills, GI Joe, Nightmare, Strange Confessions, Weird Adventures, Weird Thrillers*

WHAT TO LOOK FOR

Lurid Horror, Crime, and other pre-Code comics; "Atomic War" covers, Science Fiction titles with cool covers, especially those with Planet Earth or Saturn); DC Heroic titles; early Archie titles in better than

Black Cat Mystery #50 (Harvey, 1954), CGC NM- 9.2. Bob Powell and Sid Check interior art, **$6,273.75**.

average condition; anything EC in better than average condition. TV and Movie related titles like *I Love Lucy* (Dell) and *Leave it to Beaver* (Dell) can command high prices when in exceptional condition. Atlas "Monster" comics often have great art by Jack Kirby, Steve Ditko, and others. *World's Finest Comics* #71, with the first Superman-Batman team, is a tough find that sells well.

WHAT TO AVOID

Most funny animal, with the exception of *Pogo Possum* (Dell) and selected Dell Disney titles with Carl Bark art; most Westerns; most Teen titles other than Archie-related; later Code-Approved Romance. Tarzan and other Jungle titles in anything but like-new condition are hard to sell.

Tales of Terror Annual #1 (EC, 1951), CGC VG+ 4.5. First Tales of Terror Annual, cover by Al Feldstein, **$2,868.**

The Vault of Horror #12 (#1) (EC, 1950), CGC VF 8.0. It is difficult to overstate the significance of this issue - it ties with sister title *Crypt of Terror's* #17 as the first horror comic. Johnny Craig did the cover and contributed interior art, as did Al Feldstein and Harvey Kurtzman, **$5,377.50.**

The Crypt of Terror #17 (EC, 1950), CGC NM+ 9.6. The first issue of this title carried over the numbering from *Crime Patrol*, where two issues previously, *The Crypt Keeper* and *The Crypt of Terror*, had been introduced. This was in effect the first EC New Trend title to hit the newsstands in 1950, **$11,950**.

Strange Tales #1 (Marvel, 1951), FN-. Although it would later become a launch pad for "Marvel Age" characters such as Doctor Strange and prototypes of Marvel's earliest Silver Age characters, *Strange Tales* made its debut as a horror/weird fiction title with this issue, **$776.75**.

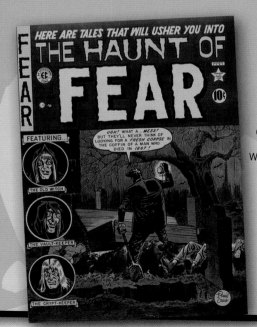

The Haunt of Fear #5 (EC, 1951), CGC NM+ 9.6. Johnny Craig cover, interior artwork by Craig, Graham Ingels, Wally Wood, and Jack Davis, **$2,151**.

Tales From the Crypt #23 (EC, 1951), CGC NM+ 9.6. This issue features an Al Feldstein cover with interior art by Feldstein, Graham Ingels, Jack Davis, and Johnny Craig, **$3,346**.

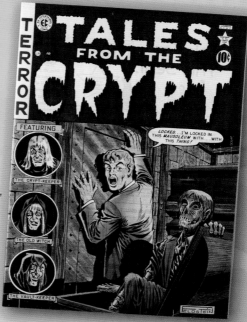

Journey Into Mystery #1 (Marvel, 1952), CGC VG/FN 5.0. Premiere issue of one of Atlas/Marvel's longest running series of the 1950s-60s, cover by Russ Heath, **$2,270.50**.

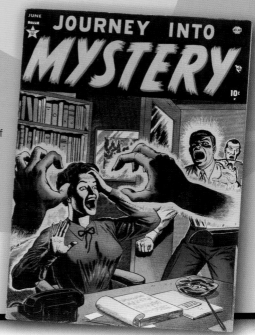

Nightmare #2 (Ziff-Davis, 1952), VF/NM. This issue's got an adaptation of Edgar Allan Poe's horror classic, "The Pit and the Pendulum," drawn by Everett Raymond Kinstler, **$1,075.50**

The Phantom Stranger #4 (DC, 1953),
GD/VG. Carmine Infantino cover, Murphy
Anderson and Joe Giella art, **$131.45**.

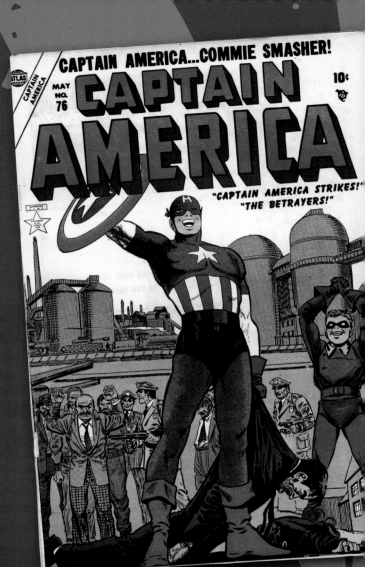

Captain America Comics #76 (Atlas, 1954), VF+.
Has a great "commie-smashing" cover by an
unknown artist, plus story art by a well-known
artist, John Romita Sr. The Human Torch and Toro
also appear, **$2,868.**

Weird Science #15 (EC, 1952), VF+. Dinosaur cover by Wally Wood, art by Wood, Al Williamson/Roy Krenkel, Jack Kamen, and Joe Orlando, **$507.88**.

Four Color #999 *Leave It To Beaver* - File Copy (Dell, 1959) CGC VF/NM 9.0, photo cover, **$262.90**.

Showcase #9 Superman's Girlfriend Lois Lane
(DC, 1957), CGC FN/VF 7.0. Lois Lane was
the first Showcase character to get her own
book, in a time when such honors were seldom
bestowed, **$1,792.50**.

The Flash #105 (DC, 1959), CGC NM
9.4. This is the first Silver Age issue
of the series, **$38,837.50**.

Tales of Suspense #39 (Marvel, 1963), CGC NM+ 9.6. The first appearance and origin of Iron Man, this issue has seen steady increases in value over the past few years thanks in part to the character's numerous adventures on the silver screen. The iconic cover is by Jack Kirby, with interior art by Don Heck and backup feature art by Steve Ditko and Gene Colan, **$262,900**.

CHAPTER 5

The 1960s

If the 1940s are considered the Golden Age of Comics, the 1960s were surely the Golden Age of Comic Fandom. Once thought of strictly as throw-away entertainment for children, comic books were now beginning to be openly collected among adult fans (most of whom were children of the '40s). Comic book conventions started to appear in the sixties, filled with small but enthusiastic crowds of older collectors, young fans, and dealers with old books to sell. The world of comic book collecting as we now know it began here, and this period is known by serious collectors as The Silver Age.

The early sixties also mark my personal involvement, beginning at age eight. After seeing comic books owned by older cousins and friends, I joined the growing ranks of comic fans in 1961 with my first comic book purchase – *Batman Annual* #1. DC became my first comic love, and I found myself spending all my allowance money on Batman, Superman, and other DCs, including a great new comic called *Justice League of America* that carried on the 1940s Justice Society of America tradition by combining all of DC's major heroes. I was also partial to *World's Finest Comics* with stories starring Batman and Robin with Superman. The best of these stories included highly stylized artwork by Dick Sprang.

THE RISE OF MARVEL

By 1960, Martin Goodman's Marvel Comics seemed to be on its last legs, reduced to filling most remaining titles with monster stories (in all fairness, the sixties were a great time for monsters, as local television stations began airing old movies like *Frankenstein* and *Dracula* late on Saturday nights; all the kids loved them). Goodman's nephew and Marvel editor-in-chief Stan Lee, seeing the renewed interest in DC's once-moribund heroes, decided to give the costumed hero thing one more try. Inspired by the American Space Program, he developed a true space-age concept called Fantastic Four. With veteran artist Jack Kirby providing the visuals, it was a hit. Stan's next innovation made even a bigger impact. *Amazing Fantasy* #15 introduced Spider-Man, and all of a sudden, everyone seemed to be a comic book fan – not just the eight-to twelve-year olds that everyone assumed

1960s COMICS

1. *AMAZING FANTASY* #15 (FIRST APPEARANCE OF SPIDER-MAN)

2. *INCREDIBLE HULK* #1 (FIRST APPEARANCE OF THE HULK)

3. *FANTASTIC FOUR* #1 (FIRST APPEARANCE OF THE FANTASTIC FOUR)

4. *AMAZING SPIDER-MAN* #1

5. *JOURNEY INTO MYSTERY* #83 (FIRST APPEARANCE OF THOR)

6. *X-MEN* #1 (FIRST APPEARANCE OF THE X-MEN)

7. *TALES OF SUSPENSE* #39 (FIRST APPEARANCE OF IRON MAN)

8. *THE BRAVE AND THE BOLD* #28 (FIRST APPEARANCE OF THE JUSTICE LEAGUE OF AMERICA)

9. *AVENGERS* #1 (FIRST APPEARANCE OF THE AVENGERS)

10. *SHOWCASE* #22 (FIRST APPEARANCE OF THE SILVER AGE GREEN LANTERN)

were the only reads, but also high school and college kids who were drawn to Marvel's fresh approach. Taking a cue from TV soap operas, Stan's stories were filled with personal drama, and were almost always continued in the next issue (or even in a different title). Marvel managed to successfully revive 1940s Timely heroes Captain America, Sub-Mariner, and the Human Torch (this time around reinvented as Johnny Storm, part of the Fantastic Four), but also introduced a new slew of comic book do-gooders like Daredevil, Thor, the Hulk, and plenty more. Marvel comics from the early-mid sixties were hot, and remain so today with collectors.

Showcase #22 Green Lantern (DC, 1959), CGC VF/NM 9.0. Not only does Hal Jordan make his debut here, the book also has the first appearances of Abin Sur (the alien who gives Hal his powers) and Carol Ferris (Hal's love interest and also his boss), Gil Kane handled the cover and interior art, **$59,750**.

BATMAN ON TV: THE POP CULTURE REVOLUTION

Even though I was just becoming a fan, the Batman
comic books had become poor sellers in the early sixties.
The Science Fiction craze of the 1950s had begun to influ-
ence the character, and by 1960, the stories were more devoted to fighting strange creatures from outer space rather
than old foes the Joker and the Penguin. DC revamped the
comic in 1964, streamlining Batman's look and ditching the
old stories for detective driven tales, bringing the character
back to his roots. DC referred to the change as the "New
Look" Batman, characterized by an added yellow oval
around his chest emblem of a flying bat. They even reintroduced an old villain that hadn't been seen since 1948, the
Riddler. His reintroduction, in *Batman* #171, happened to
be seen by a television producer, who was inspired to create a new show, and on January 12, 1966, Batman starring
Adam West and Burt Ward as the "Dynamic Duo" pre-
miered on ABC-TV. It was a smash hit. Comic books had
inspired a syndicated Superman series in the 1950s (that
helped keep that helped keep the character alive during
the "lean years"), but Batman was even a bigger success.
Comic books were now important. Now is when the idea of
saving your old comic books really took hold of the nation.
As a result, there are far more survivors from 1965 and
beyond than was the average in the forties and fifties.

The Swinging Sixties is well remembered for its color-
ful, splashy look, and comic books soon were considered part of the pop culture art movement that made
a star out of Andy Warhol. The more "over the top" the
comics were with wild inventions and crazy villains (as
was the *Batman* TV series), the more "high camp" they

were considered. Marvel even briefly ran a "Pop Art Production" tagline on its covers.

OTHER 1960s PUBLISHERS

In addition to the Big Two of DC and Marvel, several other companies managed to hold on and continue to produce comic books on a regular basis. Here are the most important ones:

ACG (American Comics Group): 1960s titles include *Adventures into the Unknown, Forbidden Worlds*, and *Unknown Worlds*; these last two titles featured an unusual tongue-in-cheek character named Herbie, who became the company's biggest seller, with his own title that ran 23 issues during the 1960s.

Archie: Besides the popular teen-ager and his Riverdale pals, the Archie group also delved briefly in the superhero market with its Archie Adventure line. Titles included *Adventures of the Fly, The Jaguar*, and *The Shadow*. By the mid-sixties, the line became known as Mighty Comics, with The *Mighty Crusaders* and *Mighty Comics*, reviving old MLJ heroes like Steel Sterling, Black Hood, and Hangman. The line was discontinued in 1967.

Dell and Gold Key: Western Printing and Lithography had published the Dell comic line since the 1930s, but in 1962, they severed their relationship with Dell and created their own Gold Key imprint. Gold Key held on to licensed characters from Walt Disney and others, and expanded into fresh territory with new titles like *Magnus, Robot Fighter*, and *Doctor Solar*. They also continued adapting TV series, like *Star Trek*. Dell continued to publish, including many adaptations of TV shows like *The Beverly Hillbillies, Burke's Law*, and *F Troop*, but without the Disney franchise, they slowly faded, ceasing operations entirely by 1973.

Tower Comics: From 1965 until 1969, artist Wally Wood helmed a company that produced some innovative titles: *T.H.U.N.D.E.R. Agents, Dynamo, NoMan*, and *Undersea Agent*, plus Teen-oriented titles *Tippy Teen, Tippy's Friends Go-Go and Animal*, and *Teen-In*.

Charlton: Still considered the "poverty row" comic book publisher, Charlton actually thrived throughout the sixties. Silver Age hero Captain Atom was introduced in 1960, with art by future Spider-Man artist Steve Ditko, and Golden Age hero Blue Beetle was revived; Science Fiction titles were still being produced (*Space Adventures, Strange Suspense Stories*); early sixties monster comics were popular (*Reptilicus, Gorgo, Konga*), and the company filled the newsstands with Romance, War, TV, and Western titles.

Gilberton: Still producing *Classic Illustrated*, with the series finally ending in 1969 with issue #169.

Harvey: Humor titles like *Richie Rich, Friendly Ghost Casper*, and *Sad Sack* were huge sellers during the sixties. Harvey would eventually concentrate solely on the funny stuff by the end of the decade, but the company's Thrill Adventure and Harvey Thriller line produced a number of action/adventure and superhero titles, like *Alarming Adventures, Double-Dare Adventures, Jigsaw, Spyman, Thrill-O-Rama*, and *Unearthly Spectaculars*. Two older heroes, Will Eisner's *Spirit* and Simon & Kirby's *Fighting American*, were briefly dusted off.

Warren: This was a line of magazine-sized comic books, printed in black and white, that continued to mine the Horror vein; these were aimed at older readers. Titles include *Creepy, Eerie*, and *Blazing Combat*.

UNDERGROUND COMIX

The no-holds-barred humor of Underground Comix had its roots in the old EC's (*MAD* in particular) and college humor magazines. The genre began in earnest with *Zap Comix* #1, published in February 1968, featuring art by Robert Crumb, who signed his work as R. Crumb. This genre would explode in the 1970s.

WHAT TO LOOK FOR

Marvel hero titles, especially when in high grade, are pure gold. Even well-read copies of early *Amazing Spider-Man* and *Fantastic Four* can bring good money. Early- to mid-sixties DCs are heating up in value. Since

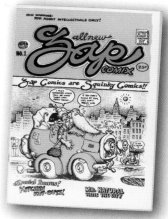

Zap Comix #1 (Apex Novelties, 1967), CGC NM 9.4. Features Robert Crumb stories, cover, and art, **$28,680**.

there were so many more who saved their comics during this time, condition does begin to get more important, especially with comics from later in the decade. The *Eighty Page Giant* issues, at one time dismissed by collectors for their reprint content, are now sought after. The first printing of *Zap Comix* #1 is an important book – look for the 25 cents cover price and the "Printed by Charles Plymell" credit line on the back cover.

Cool covers are still a good gauge to any comic's worth, and there were plenty in the sixties. DC Covers featuring gorillas, dinosaurs (especially *Star-Spangled War Stories* and the "War That Time Forgot" series), Saturn and Earth Sci-Fi covers are all sought after.

WHAT TO AVOID

Stay away from most heavily used comics; unless it's a copy of *Fantastic Four* #1 or the first issue of *Amazing Spider-Man*, hold off on anything with such obvious damage as mold, missing/cut pages, and water stains. Some humor titles are important, but there were hundreds of different *Richie Rich* comics, with only a few having much value. Gold Key action/adventure titles can be collectible, but only in high grade; the same applies for most Charlton titles as well. *Archie* comics are plentiful from this era, so stick with the high-grade copies; most other publisher Teen-oriented and Romance titles have little value, even those published by DC and Marvel.

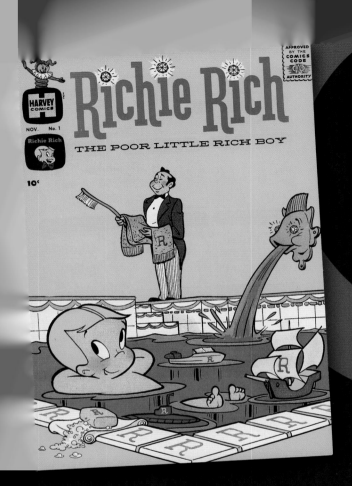

Richie Rich #1 (Harvey, 1960), CGC NM+ 9.6.
It could be said that this issue started the whole
Richie Rich phenomenon. While the Poor Little Rich
Boy had been a backup feature in every issue of
Little Dot, and had two Harvey Hits tryout issues
devoted to him, this series proved that he could
carry his own book. Warren Kremer provided the
visuals for this early outing, **$29,875**.

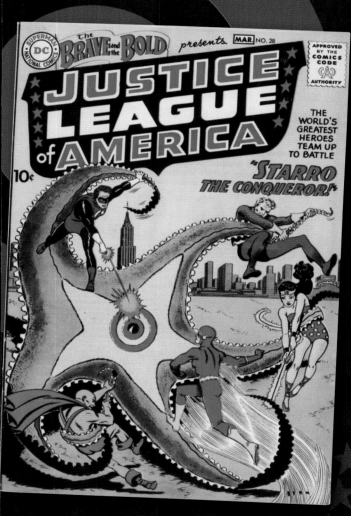

The Brave and the Bold #28 *Justice League of America* (DC, 1960), CGC VF/NM 9.0. This is the first appearance of the Justice League of America, **$31,070**.

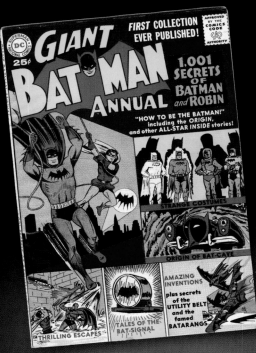

Batman Annual #1 (DC, 1961), FN-. One-page "Secrets of Batman's Utility Belt and Famed Batarang's" feature, Curt Swan cover, **$107.55**.

Batman #171 (DC, 1965), CGC NM+ 9.6. The issue is the first Silver Age appearance of the Riddler; not only was this his first appearance since 1948, it was the issue that "made" the character. Rumor has it that when William Dozier, who became the producer of the Batman TV show, first got his hands on a copy of a Batman comic, it happened to be this issue, which is why the semi-obscure villain was the featured baddie in the very first episode of the TV show, **$16,132.50**.

Fantastic Four #1 (Marvel, 1961), CGC NM- 9.2. The origin and first appearance of the Fantastic Four, Marvel's first superhero team, with cover and interior art by Jack Kirby, **$203,150**.

Adventures of the Fly #21 (Archie, 1962), VF+, **$19**.

Strange Suspense Stories #58 (Charlton, 1962), NM-, **$120.75**.

Amazing Fantasy #15 (Marvel, 1962) CGC VF/NM 9.0. Spider-Man makes a dramatic entrance on the cover of this issue, his first appearance and origin, **$191,200**.

The Amazing Spider-Man #1 (Marvel, 1963), CGC NM 9.4. This is the first issue of the most collected title in comics, with first appearances of John Jameson, J. Jonah Jameson, and the Chameleon. Jack Kirby and Steve Ditko cover, Ditko art, **$107,550**.

Journey Into Mystery #83 (Marvel, 1962), CGC NM 9.4. The first appearance of Thor, **$179,250**.

The Incredible Hulk #1 (Marvel, 1962), CGC NM- 9.2. In addition to the origin and first appearance of the Hulk (who was gray here before becoming green in issue #2), this landmark book has the key first appearances of Rick Jones, Betty Ross, and Thunderbolt Ross; Jack Kirby provided the cover art, **$125,475**.

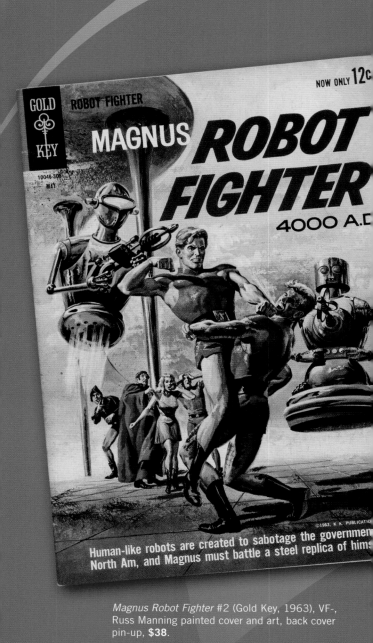

Magnus Robot Fighter #2 (Gold Key, 1963), VF-,
Russ Manning painted cover and art, back cover
pin-up, **$38**.

Herbie #1 (ACG, 1964), VG. Fidel Castro and Sonny Liston appearances, cover and art by Ogden Whitney, **$44**.

T.H.U.N.D.E.R. Agents #1 (Tower, 1965), VF. Origin and first appearance of Dynamo, Norman, Menthor, Iron Maiden, and the Thunder Squad; Wally Wood, Reed Crandall, and Gil Kane art, **$50**.

The Avengers #1 (Marvel, 1963), CGC NM 9.4.
The issue has the origin and first appearance of
the Avengers (Thor, Iron Man, Hulk, Ant-Man, and
Wasp), plus appearances by the Fantastic Four, Loki,
and the Teen Brigade; Jack Kirby cover, **$89,625.**

X-Men #1 (Marvel, 1963), CGC NM 9.4. The issue has the origin and first appearance of the X-Men (Angel, the Beast, Cyclops, Iceman, and Marvel Girl), as well as the first appearances of Professor X and Magneto; Jack Kirby provided the stellar cover and interior art, **$89,625**.

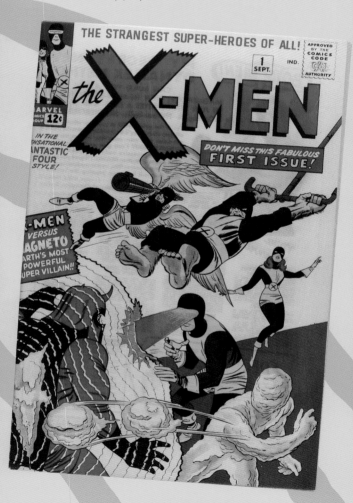

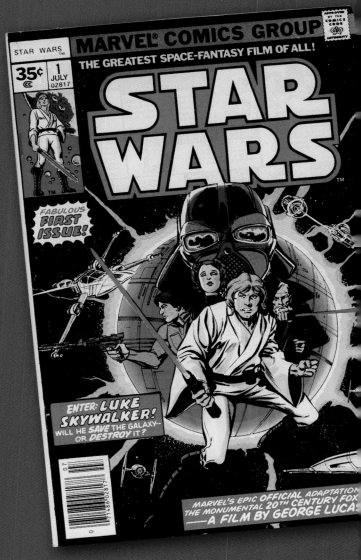

Star Wars #1 (Marvel, 1977), CGC NM 9.4. This rare 35-cent variant of Part 1 of the *Star Wars: A New Hope* movie adaptation is a Top 10 comic from the 1970s. Howard Chaykin provided the now classic cover and interior art, **$15,535**.

CHAPTER 6

The 1970s

When scrounging around for old comic books, the 1970s are the best decade to mine, with still-plentiful collections ready to be found. By this time, condition became more important than ever, with collectors vying for only copies in the best condition. CGC grading can make a huge difference, as uncertified comics worth only a few dollars can sell for hundreds in very high grade.

DC COMICS

Having lost their grip on the market to Marvel in the 1960s, DC began to show a vast improvement, with writers like Denny O'Neil and artists like Neal Adams and Bernie Wrightson coming onboard. O'Neil and Adams effectively turned the industry upside-down with their radical revamping of *Green Lantern*, starting with issue #76, in 1970. The creators took their cue from Marvel, and incorporated more human interest and relevance in a series of stories that paired right-wing, "by the book" hero Green Lantern with liberal-thinking, emotional Green Arrow. The series lasted only a few issues (ending with #89, with a few more back-up stories in *Flash*), but all the Green Lantern/Green Arrow comics are valuable, especially in high grade.

Another major innovator, Jack Kirby returned to the DC fold in the early 1970s with a big splash, beginning with his take on *Superman's Pal Jimmy Olsen*. When these issues expanded to 52 pages, old Simon & Kirby comics from DC's library were reintroduced to the public. Not all Kirby DCs from the seventies are valuable today, but high-grade copies should always be snatched up for the right price.

DC began to expand their page count from 36 to 52

pages in 1971, fill-
ing the extra pages
with reprinted
stories, sometimes
going back to the
1940s. For a while
in the mid-'70s,

most DC titles expanded to 100 pages, with even more reprinted material. All these expanded issues featured older
stories, most of which comic fans had never seen before. As
a result, interest in the Golden Age comics of the 1930s and
'40s became greater than ever, and young collectors were
now searching for comics published before they were born.

Perhaps the greatest superhero revival of all was the
much-anticipated return of Captain Marvel. DC had
won the rights to this character in the 1950s, and early
1970s interest was strong; however, the new series,
called *Shazam!* (the magic word that turned Billy Batson
into Captain Marvel), couldn't quite recapture the fun
and excitement of the original.

MARVEL

Conan the Barbarian #1 hit the stands in 1970, creating a boom in "sword and sorcerer" comics that further
impacted popular culture, resulting in big-budget movies.
Marvel's least-known 1960s superhero team the X-Men
were revamped with issue #94, after the team got a serious
makeover in *Giant-Size X-Men* #1; both of these issues, plus
a good many *X-Men* issues to follow, were wildly popular
then and highly sought-after today. Jack Kirby returned
to Marvel after his brief stay at DC, going back to Captain
America and creating new titles. A new Marvel character
seemed inspired by Donald Duck, and for a while *Howard
the Duck* was incredibly popular, but faded fast after a
lackluster feature film.

Both DC and Marvel began publishing larger-sized
comics in the mid-1970s. Roughly the size of an old *Life
Magazine*, these "Treasury" editions were difficult to

1970s COMICS

1. **STAR WARS** #1 (35 CENT PRICE VARIANT)
2. **GREEN LANTERN** #76
3. **IRON FIST** #14 (35 CENT PRICE VARIANT)
4. **CEREBUS THE AARDVARK** #1
5. **INCREDIBLE HULK** #181 (FIRST FULL APPEARANCE OF WOLVERINE)
6. **GIANT-SIZE X-MEN** #1 (FIRST APPEARANCE OF THE NEW X-MEN)
7. **X-MEN** #94
8. **HOUSE OF SECRETS** #92 (FIRST APPEARANCE OF SWAMP THING)
9. **DC 100 PAGE SUPER SPECTACULAR** #5
10. **AMAZING SPIDER-MAN** #129 (FIRST APPEARANCE OF THE PUNISHER)

TOP 10

Green Lantern #76 (DC, 1970), CGC NM/MT 9.8. The issue is significant for many reasons, including bringing Green Lantern into the modern era. Star artist Neal Adams took over as penciler of the title, and Denny O'Neil's stories brought "social conscience" to comics, taking on racism, drug addiction, and other themes, which garnered much publicity at the time, **$37,343.75**.

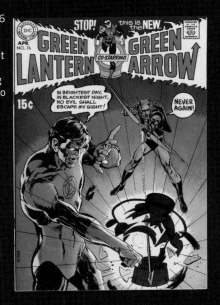

properly store without damage to the covers. Most were reprint editions; DC's *Famous First Edition* series of oversized comics is covered in Chapter 9.

OTHER MAJOR PUBLISHERS

Gold Key began to wind down in the late '70s, gradually changing its brand name to Whitman Comics (Whitman was Western Printing's children's book division). Most of the Gold Key issues from this time were reprints of earlier issues. *Harvey*, now down to just its core "Harvey World" humor titles, also began slowing down. Charlton all but gave up the ghost, after sliding sales and a loss of good talent to the better-paying publishers. *Archie* was still strong, but began shifting to digest-size editions that could be sold alongside *TV Guide* at supermarket check-outs. New company Eclipse, founded in 1977, revolutionized the industry by introducing the graphic novel concept, which boosted comic books up from the newsstands and into book stores.

THE COMIC BOOK SHOP

Speaking of newsstands and stores, stores devoted to selling comic books began popping up all over the country in the 1970s, a trend that paved the way for a major change in how comic books were distributed. In the '60s, comics were still sold along with newspapers in newsstands, drug stores, candy stores, etc. Comics were sold on a returnable basis, and any comic that was not sold after a certain time would have the top third of the cover (with the title and issue number) torn off and returned for credit. Comic store owners successfully lobbied for a new system that was more profitable, but meant no more returns, so unsold copies were saved as back issue stock. This had a serious impact on the collectability of comics in general, as now there were far more unblemished copies available for future collectors.

UNDERGROUND COMIX

These adult-themed comics with tales of sex and dope were at their height of popularity in the '70s.

BEST PICKER FIND

GREG HOLMAN: Just before I started at Heritage Auctions, I was combing used bookstores and came across a small chain of head shop/used paperbacks stores that I used to stop by every few weeks to see what they had recently gotten in. I came across a high-grade copy (VF+) of *Werewolf by Night* #32 (origin and first appearance of Moon Knight - Marc Spector). I paid 50 cents for it. In November of 2014, a CGC-certified VF+ 8.5 copy sold for $464!

However, most of the bigger sellers, like *Zap Comix*, *Fabulous Furry Freak Brothers*, and most all R. Crumb titles, were reprinted over and over again. Best not to pick these up without a copy of the *Fogel's Guide to Underground Comix*, to find out how to tell the first editions from the reprints.

WHAT TO LOOK FOR

In a word: condition. Stick to the superheroes for a sure bet, but early *Conan* and other Barbarian comics can have value. War comics, especially from DC, are often sought-after, especially when artist Joe Kubert was involved. Mystery titles are good when in high grade. Look for the 100-page DCs, as there has been growing interest in them of late. Pay attention to new comic-based movies that feature obscure characters, like the recent *Guardians of the Galaxy*, as first/early appearances can quickly go up in value.

WHAT TO AVOID

It's probably best to avoid most 1970s comics in average used condition. Superhero and action/adventure titles reigned during this time, so avoid most of the funny stuff. Some high-grade *Archies* are exceptions to this rule. The higher the cover price on regular 36-page issues, the less likely you have a valuable comic is a good rule of thumb.

Superman's Pal Jimmy Olsen #133 (DC, 1970), CGC NM/MT 9.8. The first "Fourth World" comic as Jack Kirby returned to DC, re-introduction of the Newsboy Legion, first appearance of Morgan Edge, **$806.63**.

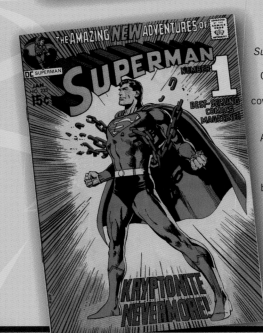

Superman #233 (DC, 1971), CGC NM+ 9.6. Neal Adams cover, Curt Swan and Murphy Anderson art. A revamping of the character begins, with Clark Kent becoming a TV newscaster, **$836.50**.

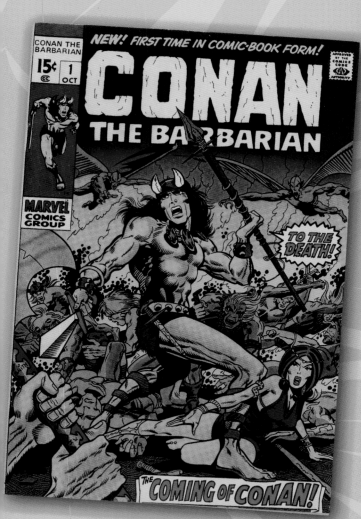

Conan the Barbarian #1 (Marvel, 1970),
CGC NM/MT 9.8. The origin and first comic
book appearance of Conan, plus the cameo
first appearance of Kull; cover and art by
Barry Smith, **$3,883.75**.

The Fabulous Furry Freak Brothers #1 First Printing (Rip Off Press, 1971), CGC VF- 7.5. Gilbert Shelton story, cover, and art, adult content, **$310.70**.

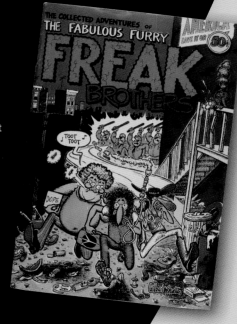

Shazam! #1 (DC, 1973), CGC NM/MT 9.8. First appearances of Captain Marvel, Captain Marvel Jr., and Mary Marvel since the Golden Age; origin of Captain Marvel retold, Superman cover appearance, Nick Cardy and Murphy Anderson cover, C. C. Beck art, **$567.63**.

House of Secrets #92 (DC, 1971), CGC NM+ 9.6. First appearance and origin of Swamp Thing, Bernie Wrightson gray tone cover and art, **$3,883.75**.

The Incredible Hulk #181 (Marvel, 1974), CGC NM/MT 9.8. The first full appearance of Wolverine seems to have cemented its status as the highest-demand 1970s comic book. Herb Trimpe is the artist of this now-famous cover, co-starring the Hulk and the Wendigo, **$26,290**.

DC 100-Page Super Spectacular Love Stories #5 (DC, 1971), CGC NM- 9.2. Cover art by Bob Oksner, **$1,135.25**.

Giant-Size X-Men #1 (Marvel, 1975), CGC NM/MT 9.8. The first appearance of the new X-Men (Nightcrawler, Storm, Colossus, and Thunderbird), this is the second most-valuable Bronze Age comic behind only *Hulk* #181, Gil Kane is the cover artist, **$6,572.50**.

X-Men #94 (Marvel, 1975), CGC NM/MT 9.8. The first issue of the regular series to feature the new team Colossus, Nightcrawler, Storm, and Wolverine, to forget past-timers Thunderbird and Sunfire. Kane and Cockrum art, **$1,847.50**.

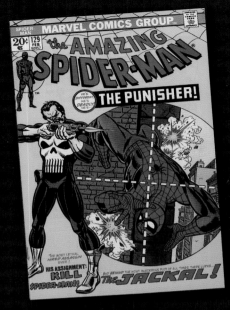

The Amazing Spider-Man #129 (Marvel, 1974), CGC NM/MT 9.8. Punisher's first appearance, also has the first appearance of the Jackal, who would figure prominently in the next 20 issues or so. Gil Kane and John Romita cover, **$14,340**.

Iron Fist #14, 35¢ price variant (Marvel, 1977), CGC VF+ 8.5. It's the first appearance of Sabretooth, one of Marvel's most fearsome villains; cover by Al Milgrom, interior art by John Byrne, **$4,182.50**.

Captain America #213, 35 cent price variant (Marvel, 1977), GD. Jack Kirby cover and art, features the Falcon. This is the scarce limited distribution 35 cent cover price variant, which is difficult to find, **$43**.

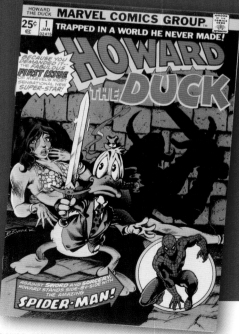

Howard the Duck #1 (Marvel, 1976), CGC NM+ 9.6. Spider-Man crossover, first appearance of Beverly Switzler, Frank Brunner cover and art, **$448.13**.

Cerebus The Aardvark #1 (Aardvark-Vanaheim, 1977), CGC FN/VF 7.0. First appearance of Cerebus the Aardvark, first Aardvark-Vanaheim comic, Dave Sim story, cover, and art, **$1,015.75**.

The Walking Dead #1 (Image, 2003), CGC MT 9.9. This is one of the hottest Modern Age books in the entire hobby, since it's the comic that started one of the hottest series currently on TV, and it also has the first appearances of Rick Grimes, Shane Walsh, and Morgan and Duane Jones. Tony Moore provided the now-famous cover and art for the book that almost single-handedly revived the zombie genre, **$8,962.50.**

CHAPTER 7

1980s and Beyond

The pickings start getting thin here, folks, when you're considering value. Most everything published from 1980 on is still in plentiful supply. There are a few exceptions, of course. We'll get to them in a bit.

The rise in stores specializing in selling comic books and related items like gaming supplies, comic-related toys, and limited edition posters, prints, and figurines gave way to a huge expansion in the industry. New companies like Pacific, First, Comico, Renegade, Dark Horse, Malibu, and Image each carved out a chunk of the market. More new comic titles were being pumped out, including a good number of black and white comics known as Independents. Most had fairly small print runs. Successful independents from the eighties include *Cerebus, Elfquest, Usagi Yojimbo*, and *Yummy Fur*.

The boom lasted through to the mid-1990s. Two events would have a huge impact on the industry and signal the end of that boom period, and both featured the Man of Steel. In 1986, DC decided to shake up sagging sales by doing to Superman what Marvel had successfully done for the X-Men, and the title was re-launched under the care of hotshot artist/writer John Byrne. The new *Superman* #1 was cover-dated January 1987, and was heavily hyped; comic shops ordered the book in bigger-than-normal numbers, encouraging their customers to buy extra copies; in short, it was an "instant" collector's item. Then, with issue #75, cover-dated January 1993, the impossible happened: the "Death of

Superman." This time, national news services took notice, and TV reports on this "end of an era" event ran on all the networks. Of course, it

would eventually all be turned around for a triumphant "return" of the character, but not before everyone and his brother trekked down to their local comic shop to buy extra copies of *Superman* #75, sealed in its cool black or white plastic bag. For a brief time, it worked: the value for #75 quickly shot up, but it didn't take long for it to drop back down; in fact, demand dropped so fast that many smaller shops wound up with boxes of unsold copies. More than a few smaller, "mom and pop" shops shut down, and in its wake, many of the independent black and white comics that had been filling shops went under as well. The boom was over.

The new companies that survived were producing the more traditional 36-page color comics, usually featuring superheroes. Artist/writer Todd McFarlane left a lucrative run on Marvel's *Spider-Man* to organize Image Comics, while former Marvel Editor-In-Chief Jim Shooter launched the Valiant line; both were initially successful, but Valiant eventually closed when parent company Acclaim shut down; it was revived a year later in 2005, on a somewhat scaled-back basis. Over at Image, McFarlane's own creation *Spawn* was initially a very hot title, with first issues briefly jumping in value, only to quickly settle down to a more modest value.

During this period, print runs shrank on most titles, even those published by DC and Marvel. Limited edition "variant" covers became a fad, with first and important key issues offered with one or more specialty covers, priced higher than regular issues. These variants can

TOP 15

1980s-2000s COMICS

A note about this list: it's still a little early for this category. Modern-era comics fall in and out of favor quickly, and this list will no doubt change several times as certain issues heat up or cool off.

1. *GOBBLEDYGOOK #1*

2. *TEENAGE MUTANT NINJA TURTLES #1* (FIRST PRINTING)

3. *GOBBLEDYGOOK #2*

4. *MIRACLEMAN #1* (GOLD EDITION)

5. *ALBEDO #2*

6. *MIRACLEMAN #1* (BLUE EDITION)

7. *VAMPIRELLA #113*

8. *GRENDEL #1*

9. *PRIMER #2*

10. *AMAZING SPIDER-MAN #1* (PLATINUM EDITION)

11. *THE WALKING DEAD #1* (FIRST EDITION)

12. *NEW MUTANTS #87*

13. *NEW MUTANTS #98*

14. *BONE #1*

15. *X-MEN #125*

Gobbledygook #1 (Mirage Studios, 1984), VF+. The first time the Teenage Mutant Ninja Turtles ever appeared in print is on the back cover of this rare issue. Even the most advanced collectors have probably never seen a copy of this comic. Fugitoid, a man's mind trapped in a robot's body, is the cover character, **$11,352.50**.

go up and come back down in value fairly quickly, but the future for these special editions is unclear. While most modern-era comics remain low value items, it's entirely possible some will soar in value someday, due to low print runs, "cool factor," or renewed interest due to movie tie-ins.

WHAT TO LOOK FOR

Not a whole lot, unless you have plenty of space to store your comic books. There are a few recent gems, though, like *The Walking Dead*. This low-print independent has been consistently well-written, and when a television series on cable became a cult hit, demand for first printing back issues, especially for certified high-grade copies, has skyrocketed. Keep an eye out for comics that have recently become TV series; not all will go up in value, but who knows what will become the next big seller. Certain *X-Men* issues can be worth $100 or more in like-new condition (issues #129 to #142 are good bets). *Amazing Spider-Man* #252 (first black costume) and #300 (25th Anniversary) sell high when in high grade.

And that's not all. Every few weeks or so at Heritage, we run across a spectacular auction performance for an ordinary comic with a fairly low NM- 9.2 value in *Overstreet*. The key is condition. I've said this before, but this really is important for 1980 and later comics: condition is everything. Well, maybe not *everything*, but that x-factor that makes one comic stand out from others of similar vintage is the key to high prices. Lately, it's been debut (or very early) appearances by minor characters that have a raised profile due to a new comic book series, or use in TV or movies, in certified grades like Mint 9.8. Figuring out what will be the next one to jump in value is a tricky thing to predict, but it helps to stay on top of pop culture trends. I would also suggest watching particular 1980s-2000s comics that are offered as separate lots in weekly auctions. A sudden spike in values in any particular issue could signal a new trend.

Primer #2 (Comico, 1982), CGC NM/MT 9.8.
The first appearance of Grendel and Argent,
Matt Wagner cover art, **$537.75**.

Since having these comics certified is the key, it's
worth your time to investigate grading services like CGC
and CBCS. Sign up for memberships and learn the ways
to submit your comics. Using the GPAnalysis website
(tracking sales of CGC-certified books) is also a good idea.

There are certainly a number of collectible comics
from the 1980s onward, but most will top out around $75.
Keep your *Overstreet* handy when looking at this stuff.

WHAT TO AVOID

Just about everything, unless you've really done your
homework (or the asking price is ridiculously low). Stick
to the older stuff for now – it's going to be a long time
most of these comics will be worth much.

...dygook #2 (Mirage Studios, 1984), VF/NM. Published
...same time as issue #1, this one is no easier to find.
...sue has the same Teenage Mutant Ninja Turtles ad
...back cover as does #1. Inside, the comic continues
...astman's and Peter Laird's Fugitoid story from #1,
...25.

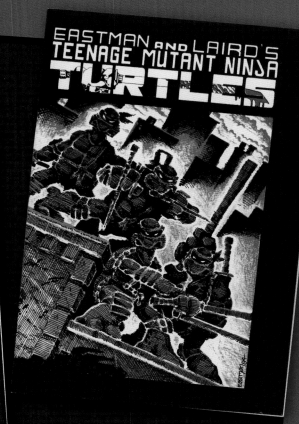

Teenage Mutant Ninja Turtles #1 First Printing
(Mirage Studios, 1984), CGC NM/MT 9.8. A
first printing copy of an increasingly hot book
featuring the origins and first appearances of
the Teenage Mutant Ninja Turtles, Splinter, and
Shredder. The wraparound cover is by Kevin
Eastman, and the story and interior art are by
Eastman and Peter Laird, **$17,925**.

X-Men #125 (Marvel, 1979), CGC NM/MT 9.8. First appearance of Mutant X (Proteus), Chris Claremont story, John Byrne and Terry Austin art, Dave Cockrum and Terry Austin cover, **$448.13**.

Albedo #2 (Thoughts and Images, 1984), CGC NM/MT 9.8. The first appearance of samurai rabbit Usagi Yojimbo is featured in this issue. The cover and art are by Stan Sakai, **$4,033.13**.

Grendel #1 (Comico, 1983), CGC NM/MT 9.8. Matt Wagner cover and art, **$597.50**.

The Saga of the Delicious Drakulonne Contin

VAMPIRELL

Vampi & Panth
go Wild in
"FEEDING FREN

VAMPIRE OF THE

Eerie Night
of Horror...
THE WAX
HOUSE

On A Nigh
of Yawnin
Graves..
TH
MUMMY'
REVENG

Vampirella #113 (Harris, 1988), CGC NM+ 9.6.
This first Harris issue had a low print run and,
consequently, is one of the most sought-after issues
by collectors, **$1,912**.

Miracleman #1 Gold Variant (Eclipse, 1985), CGC NM/MT 9.8. Story by Alan Moore, cover and art by Gary Leach, **$1,792.50**.

Bone #1 (Cartoon Books, 1991), CGC Qualified NM 9.4. Story, cover, and art by Jeff Smith. First appearances of Fone Bone, Phoney Bone, Smiley Bone, the Great Red Dragon, and Ted, **$1,123.30**.

Todd McFarlane's *The Amazing Spider-Man* #328 cover original art (Marvel, 1990). Spidey demonstrates his awesome new powers on the Hulk, and this illustration sky-rocketed McFarlane's career, **$657,250**.

CHAPTER 8

More Cool Stuff

PLATINUM AGE COMICS

The Overstreet Comic Book Price Guide notes the Platinum Age of Comics is from 1883 to 1938. Yes, there were "comic books" back then, only in a different format than the standard comic, printed mostly in a "landscape" format with thick card covers or hardbacks. Most of these early books are newspaper comic strip reprints of a certain character or strip, like *Bringing Up Father* or *Mutt and Jeff*. These generally started appearing in stores around 1900. Some older Platinum Age books featured original content. All are incredibly tough to find today, but they do occasionally turn up. Look for complete copies, but don't pass on a book due to rough shape – as long as there are no problems like water damage or mold, and no obvious missing pages or covers.

BIG LITTLE BOOKS

These were little books, roughly 3-3/4 inches x 4-1/2 inches, and usually about an inch thick, that were popular during the 1930s and '40s. A typical Big Little Book would feature text on one page, with a black and white comic panel illustration on the facing page. Some books were All Comics, with stories usually modified version of what appeared in comic books; there were a few different size formats used as well.

All manner of comic strip characters were featured, as well as original characters and even movie adaptations, with photo illustrations. The biggest publishers were Whitman (the same company that produced Dell Comics, plus other children's books) and Saalfield, but there were several others.

Condition is the key here, as these little books were not designed to hold up well. The spine areas are usually the first to go, so make sure the spine is fully attached. Finding copies of Big Little Books in like-new condition is next to impossible, so exceptionally clean, unused copies can sell for good money. *The Overstreet Comic Book Price Guide* has a section devoted to them.

NEWSPAPER COMIC STRIPS

Hardly a week goes by at Heritage Auctions without my fielding a phone call from someone who has "the last *Peanuts* comic strip," thinking that have something special. Special it may be in terms of content and history, but value-wise, next to nothing.

Collecting clipped newspaper comic strips was once a popular hobby in America, but there are few you still collect today, and fewer still willing to pay good money for the strips. All the many strip reprint books published over the past forty years probably has something to do with this, especially for the most popular comic strips, like *Flash Gordon*, *Tarzan*, and yes, *Peanuts*.

Check eBay – there, one can usually find a month's worth of clipped dailies for just about any strip you can think of, selling for as little as $5. My advice would be to steer clear of these. Very old full-page or full-section Sunday comics, when in exceptional condition, might be worth selling, but they need to be really old (before 1940) and really nice, like unfolded examples cut from bound newspaper volumes.

PROMOTIONAL COMICS

Over the years, many businesses have offered free comic books to promote their services, explain the history behind their product, or simply as a gift for the

PLATINUM AGE COMICS

1. *YELLOW KID IN MCFADDEN FLATS*
2. *MICKEY MOUSE BOOK,* SECOND PRINTING VARIANT
3. *LITTLE SAMMY SNEEZE*
4. *MICKEY MOUSE BOOK,* FIRST PRINTING
5. *LITTLE NEMO (1906 EDITION)*
6. *PORE LI'L MOSE*
7. *LITTLE NEMO (1909 EDITION)*
8. *YELLOW KID #1*
9. *BUSTER BROWN AND HIS RESOLUTIONS (1903 EDITION)*
10. *MICKEY MOUSE BOOK,* SECOND PRINTING

TOP 10

The Yellow Kid in McFadden's Flats #nn (G. W. Dillingham Co., 1897), FN/VF. The first comic book (of sorts) to feature the Yellow Kid. The 196-page square-bound publication features a narrative by E. W. Townsend with reprinted black-and-white Sunday comic-strip art by R. F. Outcault, **$4,182.50**.

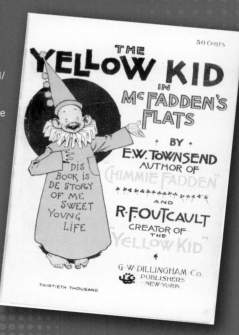

Promotional comics box lot (1930s-1980s), VF. Approximately 100 promotional comics, with the majority being high-grade, but condition varies. Issues include *All Star Dairies*; *Buster Brown Goes to Mars*; *Danny and the Demoncycle*; *Dick Tracy Sheds Light on the Mole*; *Pinocchio Learns About Kites*; *Magic Shoes and the Missing Masterpiece Mystery*; *The Gun That Won the West*; *Happiness and Healing For You*; *Fireworks Fun From Spencer*, and much more, **$2,210.75**.

kiddies, with either reprints or unsold comic books with the old cover removed and a new cover stapled on. Some giveaways can be quite valuable, especially when from the 1930s or '40s, but there have been more recent promotional comics that hold value.

Some promos, like the March of Comics small-sized booklets given away at stores, are fairly common, but certain issues are valuable. Giveaways with Disney characters are usually sought-after. Early full-size copies (with plain paper covers) starring Donald Duck, like "Maharajah Donald," "Darkest Africa," and "Race to the South Seas," are very valuable.

GAMES, TOYS, AND ACTION FIGURES

When encountering these types of items, look first for age (most will carry a copyright date somewhere), and then condition. Stay away from most modern-era toys and figures, unless they are new-in-box, and even then, it's best to do a quick check for similar items on eBay. Vintage toys are especially valuable when still with the original box, which can sometimes be as valuable as the toy itself. Most popular comic characters have related

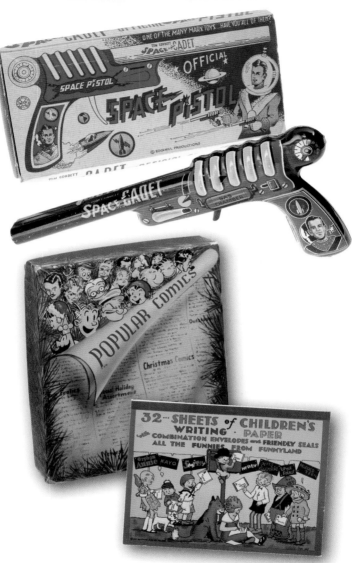

Comics-related game and card group (various, 1932-56).
This collection of vintage games, cards, and oddities has
some fascinating items including a Tom Corbett Space Cadet
1953 tin "click" Space Pistol and box, Space Patrol set of
Reed's Party Plates, 32 sheets of children's writing paper kit
including combination letter/envelopes and stamps featuring
Little Orphan Annie, Smitty, Perry Winkle, and others,
Gene Autry Stencil Book, a 1930s Mickey Mouse store ad
promoting Kolynos tooth paste, and much more, **$1,553.50**.

toys issued through the years; Buck Rogers toy guns from the 1930s remain popular with collectors today and command premium prices in just about any condition. Superman and Captain Marvel toys from the 1940s are always sought after. Radio premiums from the '40s, like Little Orphan Annie and Captain Midnight decoders, have dipped a bit in popularity, but still sell for good prices when in above average condition. The 1966 *Batman* TV series inspired a slew of Bat-toys and related products; while many are still fairly common, something like the Batman Utility Belt Crime Fighting Equipment Playset in exceptional condition (and still in the box,

complete with all parts), are highly desired (Heritage sold a set in 2012 that went for $5,676.25).

Games are generally to be avoided unless (1) they are old and comic-character related, and (2) if you can verify that all pieces are included, and the box is not damaged in any way. Check eBay for similar items to determine value. Some games, like Monopoly, have been issued many times, in boxes with different designs. Naturally, the older the better should be your rule of thumb. Be on the lookout for modern-day reproductions of earlier versions.

A copy of *Hake's Official Price Guide to Pop Culture Memorabilia* would be handy to have when encountering these items.

All Star Comics #1-12 bound volume (DC, 1940-42). This volume contains the first twelve issues of one of the most collectible series ever, featuring two of the 25 most valuable Golden Age books, namely #3 (first appearance of the Justice Society of America) and #8 (first appearance of Wonder Woman), **$16,730**.

GRAPHIC NOVELS AND BOOK COLLECTIONS

While the graphic novel (a new, longer comic story in book form, either softcover or hardback) has only been around since the 1980s, collected book editions of classic comic strips and comic book stories go back to the earliest days (as noted in our discussion of Platinum Age comics). Most of these book editions from the 1960s on remain common and low value, but there can be exceptions. Paperback book collections of comic strips have been popular since the 1940s, and early ones in exceptional condition are worth picking up. With the '60s, these became more common, but some, like the books

BIG LITTLE BOOKS

TOP 10

1. **MICKEY MOUSE THE MAIL PILOT** #717, VARIANT EDITION

2. **MICKEY MOUSE AND MINNIE MOUSE AT MACY'S** (GIVEAWAY)

3. **MICKEY MOUSE AND MINNIE MARCH TO MACY'S** (GIVEAWAY)

4. **MICKEY MOUSE** #717 FIRST EDITION (THE SO-CALLED "SKINNY MICKEY" COVER)

5. **DICK TRACY THE DETECTIVE** #W-707

6. **MICKEY MOUSE** #717, SECOND EDITION (THE "REGULAR MICKEY" COVER)

7. **MICKEY MOUSE SILLY SYMPHONIES**

8. **BIG PAINT BOOK** #721 (VERSION WITH 336 PAGES)

9. **MICKEY MOUSE THE MAIL PILOT** (GREAT BIG MIDGET EDITION – BRITISH)

10. **BIG LITTLE MOTHER GOOSE** #725, SOFTCOVER EDITION

featuring DC, Marvel, and other superheroes, or the EC stories from the '50s, are still hot. Collections featuring humorous comics like *Peanuts*, *B.C.*, and *Andy Capp* are still pretty plentiful in average used condition.

It's been noted by several sources that the 1990s and beyond are turning out to be the Golden Age of Reprint Books, with a number of publishers turning out beautiful reprint editions of both comic strip and comic book material. While these generally are worth only cover price, the low press run of most books (like 2,000 copies) means a few climb in value quickly. A check of similar items listed on eBay is a good way to gage value, but

Mickey Mouse Book, later printing (Bibo & Lang, 1931), VF+. This is Disney's first licensed publication, and the content has song lyrics, Win Smith strip reprints, and a story telling how Mickey Mouse met Walt Disney, **$4,481.25**.

Big Little Book #717 Mickey Mouse (Whitman, 1933), VG. The historic first Mickey Mouse Big Little Book, **$155.35**.

keep in mind that anyone can set any price they want for anything; it's best to go by actual sales, rather than someone's Buy It Now price. Regardless of what they are selling for now, the better books of this nature are likely to climb in value before too long, and are worth salting back when you can pick them up cheap.

BOUND COMIC VOLUMES

Back in the day, comic publishers would often have copies of their published comic bound together in hardback books, to be used as reference. Sometimes these bound volumes make their way into private hands. Western Publishing went out of business in the 1980s, and hundreds of the company's library of bound volumes from the 1940s-60s hit the market when Western's parent company, Random House, cleared out its warehouses. These were professionally bound books, each containing 12 or so sequential issues. The outside edges of the comics were trimmed to make the books look uniform, but the comics themselves were usually high-grade file copies. DC and other companies did the same thing. For years, bound volumes were looked down on by collectors, and a good number of these bound volumes wound up being torn apart to separate the issues. Nowadays, a real love for these books has emerged. Publishers weren't the only ones who did this; some collectors have had their personal collections bound this way. When figuring the value of a bound volume, add up Good 2.0 (for privately bound book with copies in used condition) or Very Good 4.0 (for publisher file copies) Overstreet values. Technically, the comics are in Poor condition due to the trimming, but as long as the comics stay in the book, this is OK. Breaking the book up to separate the issues is not a good idea, as the trimming and resulting spine damage really will put these in the Poor category.

ORIGINAL COMIC ART

When serious collectors fill their want lists of comic books, the next logical step is to go after the original artwork used to produce the books. These are one-of-a-kind, hand-drawn pages, done larger than printed size in inks over penciled drawings. Original art makes its way to the market in several ways; sometimes fans write in and request a piece of art; sometimes the artist will keep his originals, and sell them to a dealer, or they might get passed down through the artist's family. Values can range from just a few dollars for a modern-era newspaper strip daily, to hundreds of thousands of dollars for a vintage page of comic book art. Two good ways to judge value would be to check for similar items online, either on eBay, or an auction site like Heritage, or consult the Jerry Weist *Comic Art Price Guide.*

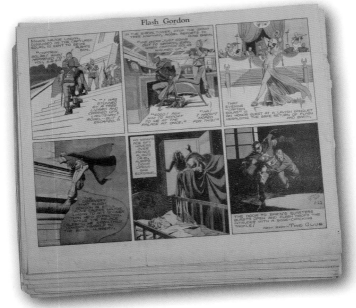

Flash Gordon half-page Sunday newspaper clipped strip group (1939), VG. Forty-four half-page color newspaper strips featuring the art of Alex Raymond; dates range from Jan. 22 to Dec. 31, 1939, **$83.65.**

Detective Comics #27 reprint (DC, 1984), CGC NM/MT 9.8.
Reprints the first appearance of Batman from *Detective Comics*
#27, 32 pages, paper cover, **$109.94**. More information about
this reprint is on P. 170.

CHAPTER 9

Reprints and Facsimile Editions

It seems like every week at Heritage I get a phone call from someone who is convinced they've found a valuable old comic book, only to learn that what they have is not that old, but in fact a reprint edition. The story usually goes something like this:

Me: Heritage Auctions, this is David. Can I help you?

Caller: Yeah, I've got a copy of the Superman comic book from April 1938.

Me: You mean Action Comics #1?

Caller: Yeah, the one where Superman is holding a car. It belonged to my grandmother, and I want to sell it.

Me: What size is it?

Caller: Oh, it's one of those large comics, like they used to sell a long time ago.

At that point, I have to tell them about the "Famous First Edition" series of oversized reprints issued by DC in the 1970s. They reprinted a number of 1930s-40s first issue reproductions back then, and unless you know what you're looking at, you could easily be fooled. In this chapter, we'll take a look at reprints and facsimile comics, and how to tell them apart from the real thing. We'll start with that first appearance of Superman, *Action Comics* #1, which has the distinction of being reprinted more times than any other issue.

The original comic book, cover-dated June 1938, hit the newsstands sometime during the late spring of that year. It was 68 pages (64 interior pages plus the covers), and included stories featuring characters like Chuck Dawson, Zatara Master Magician, Pep Morgan, and cowboy Tex Thompson. Superman was the first story in the book, and was 12 pages. The comic book measured approximately 7-1/2 inches x 10-1/4 inches, with two staples holding the book together at the spine. At right is a photo of the front and back covers of a copy, one that was graded by the Certified Guaranty Company (CGC) and certified as being authentic. There are some details on the front cover of this comic that you should note:

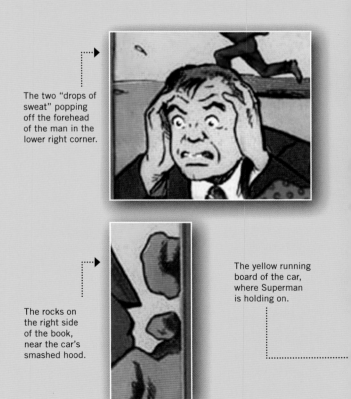

The two "drops of sweat" popping off the forehead of the man in the lower right corner.

The rocks on the right side of the book, near the car's smashed hood.

The yellow running board of the car, where Superman is holding on.

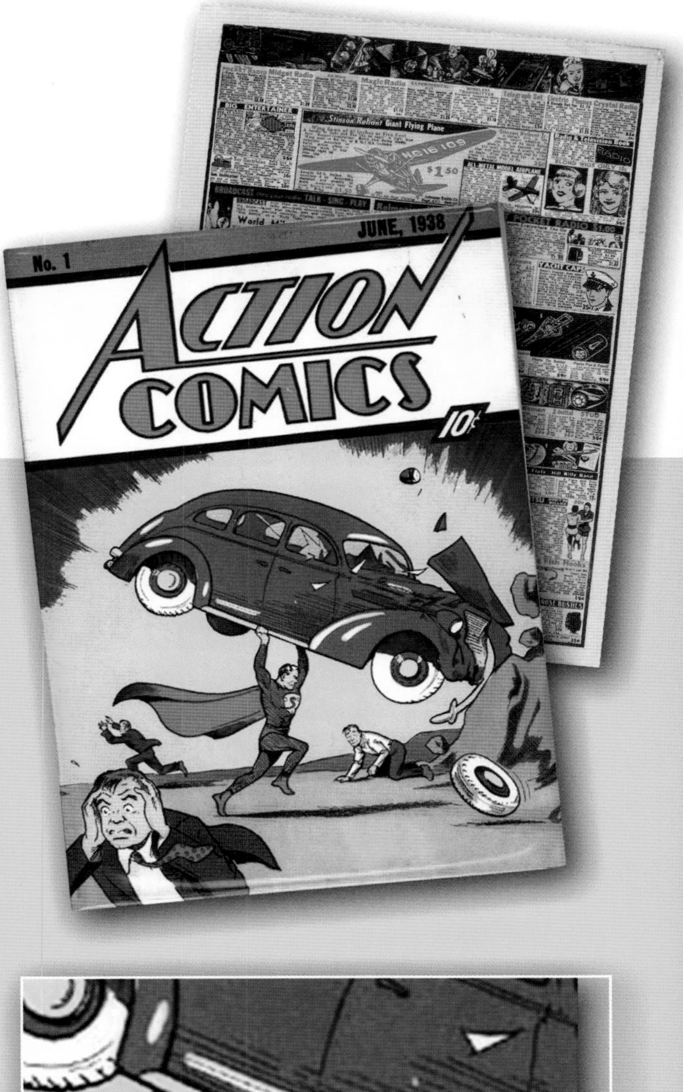
No. 1
JUNE, 1938
ACTION COMICS
10¢

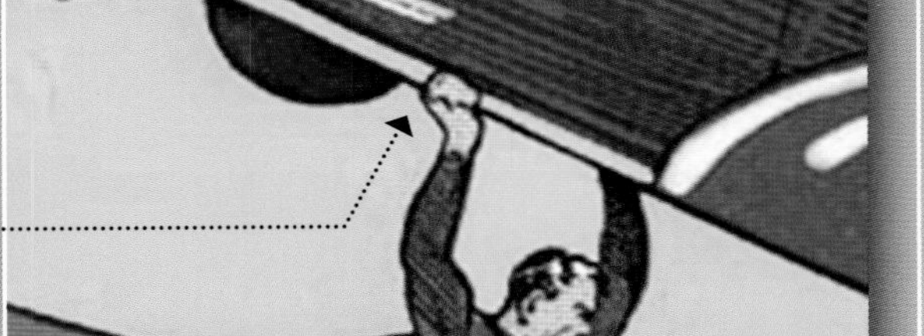

The first reprint of *Action Comics* was published as part of a series known as *Famous First Editions*. It was published with an outer cover, with the words "Famous 1st Edition" at the top of that outer cover. The outer cover of this edition was on a heavier paper stock, and was held on by three staples along the spine (instead of two). The outer covers have often been removed, leaving only the slick paper "Action" cover, making it confusing for many. Here are photos of that edition, showing the "extra" outer cover and the comic opened to reveal an inside second cover:

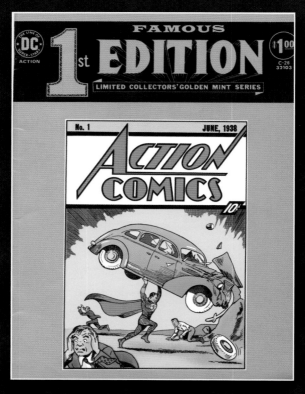

Content-wise, it's pretty much a page-by-page reprint of the 1938 edition, with one big difference: This version is oversized, measuring approximately 10" x 13-1/2".

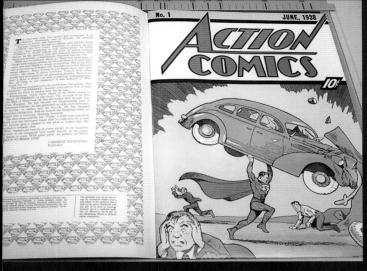

The second, inner cover is printed on slick paper and closely resembles the original 1938 comic, but with these differences:

The two "drops of sweat" are missing.

The rocks near the car's hood are missing.

The running board of the car is all green, and there are no white highlights on the front fender.

OTHER FAMOUS FIRST EDITION REPRINTS

There were a number of *Famous First Edition* comics printed in the 1970s, including *Detective Comics* #27 (first appearance of Batman), *Whiz Comics* #2 (first appearance of Captain Marvel), *Batman* #1, *Sensation Comics* #1 (Wonder Woman), *Superman* #1, *Flash Comics* #1, *Wonder Woman* #1, *and All Star Comics* #3. All were in the oversized format. Some were issued in deluxe hardcover format, and in excellent condition, these editions can be worth up to $350 each. Most of the regular editions, complete with outer covers and in excellent condition, are worth up to $90, according to the latest Overstreet comic book price guide. Problem is

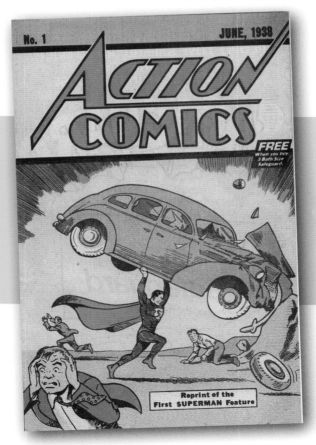

that the large size made these difficult to store without damaging; few copies are found in Near Mint condition. An average used copy, still with the outer cover, is going to have a value range of $5 to $15. When the outer cover has been removed, leaving behind the facsimile cover, there will be little or no value.

OTHER ACTION COMICS #1 REPRINTS

Other reprints of *Action Comics* #1 were smaller, closer to the size of modern comics. Most were issued as giveaways (marked "Free"), or sold with cover prices of 50 cents and one dollar. Some were priced at 10 cents, but only featured the Superman story, and were 16 pages instead of 64. These editions usually have either a picture of Superman, or the Nestlés Bunny, on the back cover. The actual 1938 edition had an advertisement for the Johnson Smith Company on the back. All carry the "June 1938" date in the upper right corner of the front cover.

Here are some notes on the other reprints:

The 1976 *Action Comics #1* 10¢ and "Safeguard" Editions:

- Has a "paper" cover (newsprint paper similar to interior pages) rather than a "slick" cover.
- Either a ten cent cover price or "Free When You Buy Two Bars of Safeguard Soap" box.
- 16 pages rather than the 64 pages of the original edition; includes only the Superman story.
- Text box on the lower right cover, with "Reprint of the First SUPERMAN Feature."

Differences in the front cover image are similar to the oversized Famous First Edition version: no orange rocks in front of the car, no yellow running board or white highlights within the green on the car, no drops of sweat flying off the man's head in the lower left. An image of Superman appears on the back cover.

The 1983/87 Nestlés Quik *Action Comics* #1 Editions:

- Both featured the Nestlés Quik Bunny
  on the back cover
- 16 pages with paper covers
- 1983 version had a ten cent cover price
- 1987 version had a fifty cent cover price

**The 1988 *Action Comics* #1 Newsstand/
Direct Sale Edition:**

- Has a slick cover
- The Newsstand version has a UPC price code
  rectangular box in the lower left corner
- The "Direct Sales" version replaces the UPC box with
  one marked "Fifty Years" and the Superman "S" logo
  Note that the "drops of sweat" man has been completely removed from the cover, replaced the rectangular
box. Superman appears on the back cover.

The 1992 "Death of Superman" *Action Comics #1*
Edition came in a shrink-wrapped package with the
*Death of
Superman* trade
paperback,
and has a $1.00
cover price.

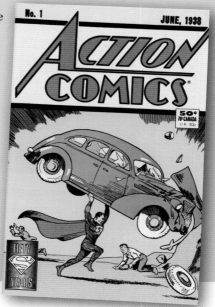

The 1998 USPS Superman Postage Stamp *Action Comics* **#1:**

- Half sheet overlay outer cover and First Day of Issue US Postage stamp featuring Superman
- 52 pages
- No price box on Action Comics front cover, $7.95 price on the overlay

The 2000 *Millennium Edition Action Comics* #1 is the easiest to spot as a reprint; the cover adds a brown background and tilts the *Action Comics* #1 cover image, which has no price box; the actual price can be found above the UPC Price Code box:

Please note that most of the *Action Comics* #1 reprints, especially the *Famous First Edition* version missing the outer cover, have little relative value. Only the *authentic 1938 version* sells for up to a million dollars and more. Also, look closely at the comic; color photocopy versions have been reported, created to fool unsuspecting buyers. So, if someone offers you a copy of *Action Comics* #1 for sale, be absolutely sure of what is being offered before you part with any money. Use a magnifying glass if needed – are there tiny red, blue, and yellow dots in areas that should be solid white?

DETECTIVE COMICS #27 AND OTHER SMALL-SIZED DC REPRINTS

In 1984, Oreo Cookies issued a regular comic-sized reprint of Batman's first appearance in *Detective Comics* #27 (shown on P. 160). This reprint is fairly easy to spot: it has a regular paper cover (not a "slick" cover) marked "Free," and has only 32 pages (the original is 64 pages), and it features not one but three different Batman stories, where the 1939 edition had only one, with other stories rounding out the comic. *Detective Comics* #38, with the first appearance of Robin the Boy Wonder was also reprinted, in 1995 by Blockbuster Videos, and in '97 by Toys R Us. Both are marked on the cover as being replica editions. A later issue of *Detective* #359 (first Batgirl) was reprinted in 1997 by Toys R Us, and is also marked on the cover, including a Toys R Us logo in the upper right corner.

In 1977, Pizza Hut released a series of DC facsimile editions of six different 1950s DC comics: *Batman* #122 and #123; *Superman* #97 and #113; and *Wonder Woman* #60 and #62. All have "Pizza Hut" marked at the top of each cover, with a Pizza Hut ad on the back covers.

In 2000, two deluxe "Masterpiece Edition" boxed sets were released featuring Superman and Batman, each including a comic reprint, a hardcover history of each character written by Les Daniels, and a small figurine. Both reprints (*Superman* #1 and *Batman* #1) are printed same size as the originals, but the interior paper is white (not newsprint), and both are marked inside as facsimile editions.

MARVEL COMICS REPRINTS

Pizza Hut also issued six different *X-Men* reprints in 1993, plus four *Real Heroes* titles in 1994 featuring Marvel characters; all are identified on the front covers as from Pizza Hut. Golden Records issued several key Silver Age Marvels in book and record sets, reprinting *Amazing Spider-Man* #1, *Journey Into Mystery* #83 (Thor), *Avengers* #4 (with Captain America) and *Fantastic Four* #1. All are identical reprints with one big exception: no price listed on the covers (NOTE: These reprints, when found still inside the sealed

Picker's Tip

When taking a comic book out of a protective plastic bag, be sure to take the tape completely off the back flap, and stick somewhere where it can be reused, but will not touch the comic itself. A tape "snag" on the front cover can drastically lower the value of a comic.

record albums, can still be quite valuable). In 1994, a set of 15 "second printing" Marvel comics were issued together as a "Vintage Pack" and sold through J. C. Penny; comics included *Amazing Adult Fantasy* #13; *Amazing Spider-Man Special* #5; *Avengers* #88; *Captain America* #109; *Fantastic Four* #66 and 67; *Incredible Hulk* #140; *Sgt. Fury* #13; *Sub-Mariner* #8; *Thor Special* #2; *Tomb of Dracula* #25; *Uncanny X-Men* #28, 62, and 63; and *Young Men* #25. These reprints look pretty convincing on the front cover, but inside, they are marked as "Second Printing" and have new advertisements for Bic Pens and Strydex.

Spider-Man's first appearance in *Amazing Fantasy* #15 has been reprinted several times, including 2002, as part of a DVD set. In 2006, newspapers all over America issued a series of 16-page Spider-Man "Collectible Series" reprint editions (including a version of *Amazing Fantasy* #15), one per week for 24 weeks. These all have "Not For Resale" listed on the front covers, and generally are worth $2-5 each when in like-new condition.

GOLDEN AGE "FLASHBACK" REPRINTS

Alan Light was the publisher of an early comic book collector newspaper, *The Buyer's Guide* (later known as *Comic Buyer's Guide,* or *CBG)*. In the 1970s, he issued a series of Golden Age comics reprints he called *Flashback Editions*. These were the same size as the original comics with color covers and all pages reprinted, but instead of printing in color on newsprint paper, the interiors were in black and white on white paper. The printing resembles Xerox copies, grey and sometimes faded-looking. The covers have the usual 10 cent prices (some as 15 cents), selling them for $10 each. Here's a list of *Flashbacks*:

- *Daredevil Comics* #1, aka *Daredevil Battles Hitler* (Lev Gleason)
- *Special Edition Comics* (Captain Marvel)
- *USA Comics* #1
- *Special Comics* (featuring Hangman)
- *Military Comics* #1
- *All Star Comics* #1, #2, #3, #4
- *Pep* #1 and #17
- *Young Allies* #1
- *Dollman Quarterly*
- *Captain Marvel Adventures* #1, #2, #7
- *Plastic Man* #1
- *World's Fair Comics* 1939 (Superman and Batman, yellow cover)
- *All Select* #14
- *Captain Marvel Jr* #1
- *Master Comics* #21
- *Sub-Mariner Comics* #1
- *World's Fair Comics* 1940 (light blue cover)
- *Human Torch* #1
- *All Winners* #1
- *Spy Smasher* #1
- *America's Greatest Comics* #1
- *Marvel Mystery Comics* #4
- *Silver Streak* #6
- *World's Finest Comics* #7
- *Captain America* #2
- *All American* #24
- *Hit Comics* #1

Flashback Group (Funnies Publishing Co., 1973-76), Average NM-. Includes #1 (reprints *Daredevil Comics* #1), 2 (*Special Edition Comics* #2), 4 (*Special Comics* #1), 5 (*Military Comics* #1), 9 (*Doll Man Quarterly* #1), 11 (*Plastic Man* #1), 17 (*Captain Marvel Jr.* #1), 18 (*Master Comics* #21), 19 (*Sub-Mariner Comics* #1), 20 (*New York World's Fair Comics* 1940), 22 (*All-Star Comics* #1), 24 (*Spy Smasher* #1), 25 (*America's Greatest Comics* #1), 27 (*Silver Streak Comics* #6), 32 (*America's Greatest Comics* #7), 33 (*Plastic Man* #2), and 34 (*Ibis the Invincible* #1), **$250.95**.

- *America's Greatest Comics* #7
- *Plastic Man* #2
- *Ibis The Invincible* #1
- *Flash Comics* #15
- *Captain Midnight* #1
- *World's Finest Comics* #8
- *Wow Comics* #1
- *Silver Streak* #1
- *Blackhawk* #9
- *Police Comics* #1
- *Uncle Sam Quarterly* #1
- *Whiz Comics* #2 (#1)
- *Air Fighters* #2

Remember, Flashback issues all have black and white (not full color) interior pages.

This list is not complete, but most other reprints are easy to tell from the original editions, if you look closely. Notice the added border around this 1993 Marvel reprint of *Amazing Spider-Man* #1, part of their "Marvel Milestone Edition" series, shown below.

In addition, both Marvel and DC regularly reprinted old stories, sometimes in a thicker "annual" comic with 68 to 100 pages, sometimes as a standard 32-page issue, but always with new cover art and titles. These types of reprints can have value, especially the older issues and those in high grade. Look in the *Overstreet Comic Book Price Guide* for individual values.

Marvel Milestone Edition:
Amazing Spider Man #1
(Marvel, 1993), CGC NM/MT
9.8, reprint, **$23**.

A restored copy of *Tales of Suspense* #39 married cover (Marvel, 1963), CGC Apparent GD/VG 3.0 Moderate/ Extensive (C-4). The origin and first appearance of Iron Man (Tony Stark), cover by Jack Kirby and Don Heck, art by Heck, Steve Ditko, and Gene Colan. Restoration includes color touch, pieces added, tear seals, reinforced, staples replaced, **$1,015.75**.

CHAPTER 10

Restoration & Repair

One thing any good comics picker must know is how to spot amateur restoration. In the sixties and seventies, it was common practice by some to use colored markers, tape, and other methods to make a worn comic book cover look better. Here are some of the things to be on the lookout for:

Color Touch: This is the use of color markers to fill in color breaks caused by creases or scuffs. Many comic books have a black line running the length of the spine; since the spine area is usually the first to show wear, this is the first place to look for touch-ups. You can spot color touch by holding the comic up to a light source; the printed colors will usually appear glossy, while the area that has been touched up will have more of a matte appearance. It sometimes helps to look at the white areas on the inside covers, as the color markers usually bleed through.

Tape Added: Finding tape on the outside cover is easy, but also check the inside covers. Some comic books have had detached covers and split spines repaired from the inside and then reattached, so check the inside covers, especially corners and spines. Tape can also be used to repair tears within the interior pages. As centerfolds are prone to come loose, some amateur repair artists will add a small piece of tape along the staple holes, from the back side, and then open the staples, press the taped area through the staples, and then bend the staples back.

Paper added: When a cover has a corner torn off, a piece of similarly-colored paper can be taped from the inside; usually, this is pretty easy to spot, especially when you open up the book and look at the inside covers.

Trimming: Some comics have rough edges along the outer edges that have been repaired by using a professional paper cutter to trim off a tiny bit from each affected side. This can be hard to spot. Comparisons with another copy can help, but the difference in size is hardly noticeable. If the exposed page edges look particularly bright and clean, this may be an indication.

Staples replaced or added: Rusty staples can be removed and the book carefully restapled. The new staples will be very new-looking, whereas an old staple will have more of a dull finish, but this isn't always an indication that they have been replaced. Look closely at the staple holes, both along the outside spine and inside the book, in the centerfold. It's nearly impossible to line up the new staples with the old holes. Also, if the staple holes inside the book look a little large, that could mean the staples are replacements. Added staples are much easier to spot – this is when someone has "reinforced" the book by adding two or more staples near (but not always on) the spine. This was a common practice for many years by merchants selling used comics.

Professional restoration is much more difficult to detect, and involves archival methods, such as making repairs with rice paper, and adding hand-painted detail to missing color areas on the cover. Modern day techniques are very sophisticated, including the use of "leaf casting" (adding paper using pulp

materials for inside pages, and similar glossy paper for the covers, in a process that involves forming a "slurry" of paper, water, and suction machines to fill missing areas, then drying and compressing the paper; finally, the missing images are painted in).

Fortunately, this type of professional repair work is costly, and most books that receive it are very rare, high-end comics that won't casually turn up in an uncertified state. Any professional restoration will be noted by the grading service.

Spotting Amateur Restoration

Here's a not-too-bad copy of an old 1940s Timely comic. But take a closer look.

Open the comic and look at the edge along the inside front cover: Someone has tried to seal tears with glue or epoxy, which has left a stain.

Now close the cover and look at the lower left corner: While it still looks a little ragged, you can tell someone tried to seal a few tears with glue.

Now here's a "really nice" 1940s *Superman*:

Not too bad, right? Tempted to give it a high grade? Take a closer look at the lower inside cover corner:

When Dad and M‹
Christmas, you be
don't delay—send ‹
rama with all the ‹
Dad and Mother a‹
have. Tell them ab‹
Fork, Cycelock and‹
extra-fun and extra‹
a Schwinn-Built, t‹
so send a postcard‹

Sch‹

SUPERMAN published ‹
Post Office at New Yor‹
1941 by Superman, In‹
entirely imaginary and ‹

You can tell by the difference in color that someone has tried to replace worn or torn paper to give the corner a sharp edge.

Look at the lower left corner on the back cover: Again, missing paper has been replaced. They even went to the trouble of drawing in the black line of the Daisy ad's outline. A pretty nice job by amateur standards, but still enough to knock down the value.

Here's another *Superman,* this time from the 1960s.

In this detail shot of the front cover, note the printed black line that runs along the spine:

Look on the inside cover, and you can see where the marker bled through a little:

You can see where that line has been touched up with a black fine-line marker.

Take the time you need to spot these problems when examining comics in the field.

WHEN SHOULD COMICS BE PROFESSIONALLY RESTORED?

For the most part, *never*. Most comic books will be worth more in their current, unrestored condition, and the majority of collectors today are interested only in unrestored comics.

A comic book that has been restored from an average Good 2.0 grade to a Very Fine 8.0 appearance may only be worth that original Good value, so costly restoration will not be worth the time, effort, and money spent. The only time I would recommend professional restoration is on a comic you plan on keeping for yourself. If reselling the book is your goal, keep it as you find it.

If you do want to go the restoration route, consider these points: the comic book should be in Very Good condition or less – nothing in better grade; the comic should be dated no later than 1963. Copies in poor or extremely brittle condition are not good candidates. Excessive tape repair, water damage and other staining, and sun fading are hard defects to repair, and should not be attempted.

Restoration by a professional can include conservation work, including removing dirt, (sight stains, and tape) and cleaning. This type of restoration will run $74 to $300, depending on the amount of work done. Leaf casting and color touch can add to the total cost, which can run up to $3,000 or more. If you go this route, use a well-known, well-established firm like CCS (Classic Collectible Services, www.ccspaper.com). Turnaround time can take up to 12 weeks, depending on the service.

Sometimes, a vintage, highly desirable comic that still has a lot of great eye appeal, but is torn along the spine area can actually benefit from tape repair. A professional archivist can use special tape to repair the cover from the inside, and then have the book CGC or CBCS graded; the tape will be noted on the grade card within the holder, but the book will not receive an "Apparent" or "Restored" notation. Consult a professional about this – never try to do it on your own.

PRESSING

Comic books found with bad bends, spine rolls, dents, cover wrinkles, folds, and other minor problems can be fixed by pressing. This must be done by a professional service, like CCS. They use professional equipment to do a proper job. Improper pressing can result in even more problems, like adding waviness and warping. Pressing and dry cleaning (which is included in pressing services) is not considered restoration by CGC and CBCS grading services, and a good professional pressing job is virtually undetectable. Pressing fees can range from $12 to $80 or more, depending on the value of the comic and amount of cleaning/pressing that is required.

A comics dealer is ready to make a sale at a
2015 convention in Dallas.
Photo by Dave Mercer

CHAPTER 11

Where to Find Comics

When I was a young comic collector back in the 1960s, I had little trouble finding old comics. A little grocery store down the street from where I lived in Houston almost always had a stack of old comics for sale, priced at a nickel apiece. I knew of several book stores that had cheap used comics for sale. Friends and relations would also on occasion give me a stack of second-hand comic books, because they knew I liked them.

Today, it's a lot tougher to locate old comics; not because all the good old ones have been found – here at Heritage, we still manage to uncover collections dating back to the 1940s on a regular basis. The problem is, so many people have heard old funny books can sell for huge sums that even worthless comics are being snatched up and saved, in hopes of a big payoff. People are cautious now, in fear of being taken advantage of by some slick dealer who buys the books for pennies, and turns around to make a big profit on them. Tracking down these old treasures at reasonable prices is difficult, but not impossible.

What usually happens these days is that someone will find a box of old comics left by a relative when that person passes on, and their house is cleaned out. Estate sales can be a good place to check. Also, abandoned storage units can be the source for a collection. Usually, the bargains to be found involve buying the entire collection for one price. When these sellers start trying to sell individual comics, they have it in their mind that everything is valuable – there may well be some value, but

chances are if they are savvy enough to sell piecemeal, they have a pretty good idea what they are worth.

Yard and garage sales can be a great source for old comics, but these will likely be issues from 1980 and later. There are so many of these comics still around, so this will be what you see the most often. Go for only the copies that are in like-new condition.

I've had luck shopping flea markets in the past twenty years, but with the advent of eBay, these honey holes are pretty well dried up by now. Still, it doesn't hurt to look if you have the time. Smaller towns in rural areas will be the best place to check for good indoor flea markets. The trick here is in knowing what to look for. If you can find a box of comics all priced the same, dig through them, and you may well find some bargains. When the prices vary book to book, that's a sure sign that someone has done their research, and will have a fairly good idea what they are worth. Keep this in mind, though: Comic book price guides change year to year, and someone may be using an outdated guide to price what they have.

Above and at left, Marvel and DC artist Sam de la Rosa mans his booth, meeting fans and selling signed items, at a 2015 comics convention in Dallas.
Photos by Dave Mercer

Running ads in newspapers and craigslist can work for you if you're in a larger city. Often, people know they have some value in the comics they've found or inherited, but they are in a hurry to sell, and willing to negotiate. Keep in mind that most professional comic book dealers pay between 15 and 25 percent of guide value for what they buy. The dealer knows he may have to hang on to the items for a while before he can make a profit on them. That percentage will rise for the right collection, as the dealer figures he can sell better quality merchandise much faster. It's all about supply and demand – if that demand is high, the supply will dwindle fast.

Shopping on eBay is a little risky, but you can on occasion get a bargain. The pros to eBay are no physical running around, no gas spent on searching; it's an easy process. The downside is that most sellers there have a good idea what they should be getting. Weekly online auctions on sites like Heritage can also be good places to check. Often, groups of comics are sold by the box, at prices that are close to wholesale. The smaller the auc-

Comics, comics, and more comics, all for sale. Who knows what treasures lie buried in these boxes? *Photo by Dave Mercer*

tion company, the better your chance will be of getting good material that can be resold at a profit; the more people bidding, the higher the final price, so it helps to go for smaller auctions.

Don't forget to ask around. Networking is a good idea – ask your friends and relations if they know of anyone with old comic books. If you wind up with a collection this way, be sure to pay fair dealer's rates, and give that person who helped you find the comics a "finder's fee" of some sort.

GOING TO COMIC CONVENTIONS

For years, a Comic Book Convention was one of the best places to find old comics. These days, the emphasis has shifted towards celebrity guests and merchandise ranging from gaming supplies to double edge swords, but most shows still feature booths loaded down with comics. While it may seem like everything at a show like this is going to be priced on the high end, the Dedicated Picker will be able to find a few bargains. Here are some hints on navigating through a con:

Look for marked-down prices. A dealer with have his best stuff up on a stand display, and boxes of mid-range comics on top on his table. But check underneath for the

Above, convention picking. At right, a line of "bargain boxes."
Photos by Dave Mercer

low-end stuff. Many dealers still carry boxes of overstock inventory to be blown out at a show, for as little as a quarter to a dollar apiece.

Most dealers are willing to negotiate their prices, especially toward the end of the day or (better yet), the end of the show. Don't be a "nickel-knocker" and try to get them to come down on a single big ticket book, but grab a few lower priced comics and ask for a better deal.

Get there as early as possible, and stay late. Be friendly, and ask how well business is doing. Many comic book dealers are a little grumpy and will complain loudly to anyone listening about how bad business has been, so be prepared for that; however, someone easy going may appreciate your chatting with them and give you a good deal on what you pick up.

Display good con etiquette. Try not to laugh at all the poorly made costumes, and don't ogle the nearly-naked girls "dressed" as Poison Ivy or other characters! Know that it may take some doing to make your way down an aisle crowed with fans, especially at larger shows like the annual San Diego Comic Con. And wear comfortable shoes!

CHAPTER 12

Selling Your Comics

For most pickers, this is going to be your main goal: Convert your finds into cash. While there are many ways to sell, there are also a few areas to avoid.

AUCTION SERVICES

Obviously, when you are lucky enough to find something really valuable, a good auction house will be a great way to go. Since I've spent the last twelve years working at the comics division of Heritage Auctions, I'm going to be a little partial to them when it comes to the best of the best. A good service should offer a great on-line presence, with easy-to-use web pages, and Heritage has one of the best. Currently, the average seller's fee charged by Heritage is 15 percent of the "hammer" price – the final winning bid. Consignments need to add up to at least $5,000 total group value – it can be one book or a box full, as long as the current market value is $5K or more. Settlement checks are written and mailed 45 days after the end of each auction. I can assure you that Heritage is an honest, "by the book" auction service, at least as far as I've observed all these years I've been with them. I've auctioned my own items with the company, and no doubt will do so again. The company offers weekly internet auctions year-round, and four major auctions with live, open to the public sessions and full-color printed catalogs. Thousands of people check out the website every day and place bids.

However, it would be a disservice to you to tell you not to check out the other major auction houses as well. It's up to you to negotiate the best deal, but keep in mind that other services may have hidden fees, so make sure all that is covered upfront with the contact person you are dealing with. Depending on what you are selling, a smaller auction house could be the best fit for you (see the list of Auction Houses at the end of the chapter).

Smaller value lots may be better sold elsewhere, though. For some, eBay is a good way to sell, and no doubt many reading this book have been selling on eBay for years. Keep in mind that when listing in an auction, keep that opening price as low as possible. Don't scare away bidders by starting too high.

CERTIFICATION OF YOUR COMICS

For any comic book that has a currently listed value of $200 or more, having it professionally graded and certified is an important option. The cost of grading varies – there are different tiers of service available, with lower fees for longer turnaround time. Currently, we at Heritage use two services, both located in Florida.

CGC, or Certified Guaranty Company has been in business since 2000, and was the first to independently act as a third party grading service. Former founder of CGC, Steve Borock, has recently begun a competing service, CBCS. Both services are highly competent, and offer trustworthy and impartial certification services. There are a couple of others out there, but I can only recommend CGC and CBCS.

A special note: If you are planning on using a large auction house to sell your comics, check with them before submitting to the graders; they may be able to handle this for you, and at a discounted rate.

SELLING TO A COLLECTOR

This is, of course, the ideal way to get the most for your comics. Finding that collector is the tough part. Unless you have lots of collector friends, the only ways to contact a collector directly is to advertise, either in trade papers, local newspapers, or an online service, you'll have to set up at a comic convention. That can be tricky – there are usually waiting lists to set up at major shows like San Diego; you better know what you're selling well (having books certified will help), and the overhead costs can be high, especially if you need to travel and stay at a hotel.

Posting info about your comics on Facebook may be a new way to reach collectors, even if your Facebook Friends are not into them, they may know of someone who is. Networking is always a good idea.

OTHER WAYS TO SELL

For lower-value comics, try a free website like eCrater.com, where you post your items with a set price (be sure to price a little under the *Overstreet Guide*, unless you are in no hurry to move the books). You can go the flea market route, or even put them in a yard/garage sale; if you do, it's best to post some sort of advertisement, in your newspaper's classified section, or online. Be vague about what you are selling – just say something like "vintage comic books for sale." Be sure to price the comics high enough to allow

you some dickering room – if you have something you think should bring $5, price it at $8 or $10, and let your customer "talk you down" a bit. He'll be happy, you'll be happy.

SELLING TO A COMIC BOOK STORE

Rarely a good idea, unless you have no money invested in the comics, and you are in a hurry to part with them. This is the easiest way to sell, but remember: most dealers pay only 15 to 25 percent of guide value. Most shops are not interested in comics from 1980 or later. They generally have plenty of those.

COMIC AUCTION COMPANIES

Heritage Auctions, 3500 Maple Avenue, 17th Floor, Dallas TX (877) HERITAGE (437-4824); www.ha.com.

Heritage Auctions, 445 Park Avenue (at 57th Street), New York NY 10022; (212) 486-3500.

Heritage Auctions, 9478 West Olympic, First Floor, Beverly Hills, CA 90212; (310) 492-8600.

ComicConnect, 36 W 27 St. FL 6, New York, NY 10018; (888) 779-7577; www.comicconnect.com.

ComicLink, (617) 517-0062; buysell@comiclink.com.

Hake's Americana & Collectibles, P. O. Box 12001 (mailing), 3679 Concord Road, York, PA 17402 (shipping); (866) 404-9800; hakes@hakes.com.

Just Kids Nostalgia, PO Box 932, Huntington, NY 11743; (631) 423-8449.

Glossary

ARRIVAL DATE: The date written (often in pencil) or stamped on the cover of comics by either the local wholesaler, newsstand owner, or distributor. The date precedes the cover date by approximately 15 to 75 days, and may vary from one locale to another or from one year to another.

ATOM AGE: Comics published from approximately 1946-1956 (some collectors consider these years as part of the Golden Age).

BONDAGE COVER: Usually denotes a female in bondage.

BOUND COPY: A comic that has been bound into a book. The process requires that the spine be trimmed and sometimes sewn into a book-like binding.

BRITISH ISSUE: A comic printed for distribution in Great Britain; these copies sometimes have the price listed in pence or pounds instead of cents or dollars.

BRITTLENESS: A severe condition of paper deterioration where paper loses its flexibility and thus chips and/or flakes easily.

BRONZE AGE: Comics published from approximately 1970 through 1985.

BROWNING: The aging of paper characterized by the ever-increasing level of oxidation characterized by darkening; The level of paper deterioration one step more severe than tanning and one step before brittleness.

CCA: Abbreviation for Comics Code Authority.

CCA SEAL: An emblem that was placed on the cover of all CCA approved comics beginning in April-May, 1955.

CENTER CREASE: See subscription copy.

CENTERFOLD OR CENTER SPREAD: The two folded pages in the center of a comic book at the terminal end of the staples.

CERTIFIED GRADING: A process provided by a professional grading service that certifies a given grade for a comic and seals the book in a protective Slab.

CGC: Abbreviation for the certified comic book grading company, Comics Guaranty, LLC.

CLASSIC COVER: A cover considered by collectors to be highly desirable because of its subject matter, artwork, historical importance, etc.

COLOR TOUCH: A restoration process by which colored ink is used to hide color flecks, color flakes, and larger areas of missing color. Short for Color Touch-Up.

COMIC BOOK REPAIR: When a tear, loose staple, or centerfold has been mended without changing or adding to the original finish of the book. Repair may involve tape, glue, or nylon gossamer, and is easily detected; considered a defect.

COMICS CODE AUTHORITY: A voluntary organization comprised of comic book publishers formed in 1954 to review (and possibly censor) comic books before they were printed and distributed. The emblem of the CCA is a white stamp in the upper right hand corner of comics dated after February 1955. The term "post-Code" refers to the time after this practice started, approximately 1955. No longer active.

COMPLETE RUN: All issues of a given title.

CON: A convention or public gathering of fans.

CONDITION: The state of preservation of a comic book, often inaccurately used interchangeably with Grade.

COVER GLOSS: The reflective quality of the cover inks.

COVER TRIMMED: Cover has been reduced in size by neatly cutting away rough or damaged edges.

COVERLESS: A comic with no cover attached. There is a niche demand for coverless comics, particularly for hard-to-find key books otherwise impossible to locate intact.

CREASE: A fold which causes ink removal, usually resulting in a white line.

DEBUT: The first time that a character appears anywhere.

DEFECT: Any fault or flaw that detracts from perfection.

DISTRIBUTOR STRIPES: Color brushed or sprayed on the edges of comic book stacks by the distributor/wholesaler to code them for expedient exchange at the sales racks. Typical colors are red, orange, yellow, green, blue, and purple. Distributor stripes are not a defect.

DOUBLE COVER: When two covers are stapled to the comic interior instead of the usual one; the exterior cover often protects the interior cover from wear and damage. This is considered a desirable situation by some collectors and may increase collector value; this is not considered a defect.

DUST SHADOW: Darker, usually linear area at the edge of some comics stored in the stacks. Some portion of the cover was not covered by the comic immediately above it and it was exposed to settling dust particles. Also see Oxidation Shadow and Sun Shadow.

ENCAPSULATION: Refers to the process of sealing certified comics in a protective plastic enclosure. Also see "Slabbing."

EYE APPEAL: A term which refers to the overall look of a comic book when held at approximately arm's length. A comic may have nice eye appeal yet still possess defects which reduce grade.

FILE COPY: A high grade comic originating from the publisher's file; contrary to what some might believe, not all file copies are in Gem Mint condition. An arrival date on the cover of a comic does not indicate that it is a file copy, though a copyright date may.

FOIL COVER: A comic book cover that has had a thin metallic foil hot stamped on it. Many of these "gimmick" covers date from the early 1990s, and might include chromium, prism, and hologram covers as well.

FOUR COLOR: Series of comics produced by Dell, characterized by hundreds of different features: named after the four-color process of printing. See One-Shot.

FOUR COLOR PROCESS: The process of printing with the three primary colors (red, yellow, and blue) plus black.

GATEFOLD COVER: A double-width fold-out cover.

GIVEAWAY: Type of comic book intended to be given away as a premium or promotional device instead of being sold.

GLASSES ATTACHED: In 3-D comics, the special blue and red cellophane and cardboard glasses are still attached to the comic.

GLASSES DETACHED: In 3-D comics, the special blue and red cellophane and cardboard glasses are not still attached to the comic; obviously less desirable than Glasses Attached.

GOLDEN AGE: Comics published from approximately 1938 (Action Comics #1) to 1945 (See Atomic Age).

GOOD GIRL ART: Refers to a style of art, usually from the 1930s-50s, that portrays women in a sexually implicit way.

GREY-TONE COVER: Also known as "wash cover." A cover art style in which pencil or charcoal underlies the normal line drawing, used to enhance the effects of light and shadow, thus producing a richer quality. These covers, prized by most collectors, are sometimes referred to as painted covers, but are not actually painted.

HRN: Abbreviation for Highest Reorder Number. This refers to a method used by collectors of Classic Comics and Classics Illustrated series to distinguish first editions from later printings.

INDICIA: Publishing and title information usually located at the bottom of the first page or the bottom of the inside front cover. In rare cases and in some pre-1938 comics, it was sometimes located on internal pages.

INFINITY COVER: Shows a scene that repeats itself to infinity.

INVESTMENT GRADE COPY: Comic of sufficiently high grade and demand to be viewed by collectors as instantly liquid should the need arise to sell; a comic in VF or better condition; a comic purchased primarily to realize a profit.

ISSUE NUMBER: The actual edition number of a given title.

KEY, KEY BOOK, OR KEY ISSUE: An issue that contains a first appearance, origin, or other historically or artistically important feature considered desirable by collectors.

LENTICULAR COVERS OR "FLICKER" COVERS: A comic book cover overlaid with a ridged plastic sheet such that the special artwork underneath appears to move when the cover is tilted at different angles perpendicular to the ridges.

LOGO: The title of a strip or comic book as it appears on the cover or title page.

MARVEL CHIPPING: A bindery (trimming/cutting) defect that results in a series of chips and tears at the top, bottom, and right edges of the cover, caused when the cutting blade of an industrial paper trimmer becomes dull. It was dubbed Marvel chipping because it can be found quite often on Marvel comics from the late '50s and early '60s, but can also occur with any company's comic books from the late 1940s through the middle 1960s.

MODERN AGE: A catch-all term usually applied to comics published from the 1980s to the present.

MYLAR: An inert, very hard, space-age plastic used to make high quality protective bags and sleeves for comic book storage. "Mylar" is a trademark of the DuPont Co.

ONE-SHOT: When only one issue is published of a title, or when a series is published where each issue is a different title (e.g. Dell's Four Color Comics).

ORIGIN: When the story of a character's creation is given.

OXIDATION SHADOW: Darker, usually linear area at the edge of some comics stored in stacks. Some portion of the cover was not covered by the comic immediately above it, and it was exposed to the air. Also see Dust Shadow and Sun Shadow.

PANELOLOGIST: One who researches comic books and/or comic strips.

PAPER COVER: Comic book cover made from the same newsprint as the interior pages. These books are extremely rare in high grade.

PEDIGREE: A book from a famous and usually high grade collection - e.g. Allentown, Lamont Larson, Edgar Church/ Mile High, Denver, San Francisco, Cosmic Aeroplane, etc. Beware of non-pedigree collections being promoted as pedigree books; only outstanding high grade collections similar to those listed qualify.

PERFECT BINDING: Pages are glued to the cover as opposed to being stapled to the cover, resulting in a flat binded side. Also known as Square Back or Square Bound.

PHOTO COVER: Comic book cover featuring a photographic image instead of a line drawing or painting.

PLATINUM AGE: Comics published from approximately 1900-1938.

POST-CODE: Describes comics published after February 1955 and usually displaying the CCA stamp in the upper right hand corner.

PRE-CODE: Describes comics published before the Comics Code Authority seal began appearing on covers in 1955.

PROVENANCE: When the owner of a book is known and is stated for the purpose of authenticating and documenting the history of the book. Example: A book from the Stan Lee or Forrest Ackerman collection would be an example of a value adding provenance.

PULP: Cheaply produced magazine made from low grade newsprint. The term comes from the wood pulp that was used in the paper manufacturing process.

QUALIFY: A Qualified grade is used when book has a significant defect that would otherwise prevent giving the highest possible grade.

RARE: 10-20 copies estimated to exist.

READING COPY: A comic that is in Fair to Good condition and is often used for research; the condition has been sufficiently reduced to the point where general handling will not degrade it further.

READING CREASE: Book-length, vertical front cover crease at staples, caused by bending the cover over the staples. Squarebounds receive these creases just by opening the cover too far to the left.

REPRINT COMICS: In earlier decades, comic books that contained newspaper strip reprints; modern reprint comics usually contain stories originally featured in older comic books.

RESTORATION: Any attempt, whether professional or amateur, to enhance the appearance of an aging or damaged comic book. These procedures may include any or all of the following techniques: recoloring, adding missing paper, stain, ink, dirt or tape removal, whitening, pressing out wrinkles, staple replacement, trimming, re-glossing, etc. Amateur work can lower the value of a book, and even professional restoration has now gained a certain negative aura in the modern marketplace from some quarters. In all cases, except for some simple cleaning procedures, a restored book can never be worth the same as an unrestored book in the same condition.

ROLLED SPINE: A spine condition caused by folding back pages while reading.

SADDLE STITCH: The staple binding of magazines and comic books.

SCARCE: 20-100 copies estimated to exist.

SEWN SPINE: A comic with many spine perforations where binders' thread held it into a bound volume. This is considered a defect.

SILVER AGE: Comics published from approximately 1956 (Showcase #4) to 1969.

SLAB: Colloquial term for the plastic enclosure used by grading certification companies to seal in certified comics.

SLABBING: Colloquial term for the process of encapsulating certified comics in a plastic enclosure.

SPINE: The left-hand edge of the comic that has been folded and stapled.

SPINE ROLL: A condition where the left edge of the comic book curves toward the front or back, caused by folding back each page as the comic was read.

SPLASH PAGE: A splash panel that takes up the entire page.

STORE STAMP: Store name (and sometimes address and telephone number) stamped in ink via rubber stamp and stamp pad.

SUBSCRIPTION COPY, SUBSCRIPTION CREASE, OR SUBSCRIPTION FOLD: A comic sent through the mail directly from the publisher or publisher's agent. Most are folded in half, causing a subscription crease or fold running down the center of the comic from top to bottom; this is considered a defect. A Subscription Fold differs from a Subscription Crease in that no ink is missing as a result of the fold.

SUN SHADOW: Darker, usually linear area at the edge of some comics in stored stacks. Some portion of the cover was not covered by the comic immediately above it, and it suffered prolonged exposure to light. A serious defect, unlike a dust shadow, which can sometimes be removed. Also see oxidation shadow.

SUPER-HERO: A costumed crime fighter with powers beyond those of mortal man.

SUPER-VILLAIN: A costumed criminal with powers beyond those of mortal man; the antithesis of Super-Hero.

3-D COMIC: Comic art that is drawn and printed in two color layers, producing a 3-D effect when viewed through special glasses.

TITLE PAGE: First page of a story showing the title of the story and possibly the creative credits and indicia.

UPGRADE: To obtain another copy of the same comic book in a higher grade.

VARIANT COVER: A different cover image used on the same issue.

VERY RARE: 1 to 10 copies estimated to exist.

VICTORIAN AGE: Comics published from approximately 1828-1899.

WANT LIST: A list of comics that a collector is interested in purchasing.

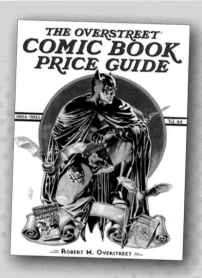

Since 1970, *The Overstreet Comic Book Price Guide* has been the definitive price guide for casual and die-hard collectors and investors alike.

The premier reference source for the hobby, the price guide is regarded for its well-researched pricing, in-depth history on comic books, and incomparable insights into the marketplace.

If you have a comic book collection or are thinking about starting one, this book should be on your shelf.

For more information, visit Gemstone Publishing, Inc., www.gemstonepub.com.

Index

Acknowledgments

Contributors to this book include Jim Steele, Greg Holman, Alex Miller, Lon Allen, Barry Sandoval, Matt Griffin, Aaron White, Jerry Stephan, Weldon Adams, Gary Dowell, and Eric Bradley.

Special thanks go out to Jim Halperin, J. C. Vaughn, Todd Hignite, Nancy Higdon, Jesus Garcia, Estella Berumen, Jennifer McDermott, Rosa Faustino, Lorena Castillo, Miguel Reynaga Sr., Simon Sanchez, and Maureen Garcia, along with Noah Fleisher, Joe and Nadia Mannarino, Ed Jaster, and Kristine Manty.

The author would like to personally thank Sonia Tosh, Alexandra Welker, Joseph Fitts, Dave Mercer, Mark Stokes, Jim Lentz, and Steve Ivy for their continued support.